RESEARCH METHODOLOGIES FOR BUSINESS MANAGEMENT

Most existing research methodologies texts take a more general approach or are edited books of previously published articles or chapters written by different authors. This book, written by a business management scholar, covers the fundamentals of business management research and its methodologies in a seamless, unified manner.

The book offers up-to-date methodologies and accessible explanations of the research process. It starts with advances in business management research methodology and gives a thorough overview on the different levels of analysis in the field. It builds upon the knowledge by examining both qualitative and quantitative research methodologies in the context of business management. It also goes over the use of machine learning and other technological advances like artificial intelligence in research and data collection, as well as how the United Nations sustainable development goals are being considered by researchers.

This book will help business management students and junior researchers quickly build an essential base of knowledge and gain a strategic advantage in publishing and reviewing business-related research.

Vanessa Ratten is Associate Professor at the School of Business, La Trobe University, Australia.

'This is a timely and comprehensive introduction to business management research methodologies which covers both qualitative and quantitative approaches to the subject. A highlight is the application of research methodologies to the United Nations Strategic Development Goals which broadens the scope of the book beyond a narrow managerial focus. There is also a useful examination of how machine learning and artificial intelligence is relevant to business management research. The author is commended for her innovative approach to this vital area of business education.'

Russell Lansbury, *Emeritus Professor and former Associate Dean of Research, University of Sydney Business School*

'Catapulted by unprecedented levels of consumer engagement, digital transformation, and vast quantities of transactional, "big" data, the research serving business management has never so desperately needed a new roadmap. *Research Methodologies for Business Management* provides a timely guide for students, academics, and practitioners to understand the transformation of business models and prosper in the new digital landscape. Its content offers a comprehensive yet accessible user-guide for every research need in the contemporary business environment. It's easy to recommend this foundational text.'

Aaron Smith, *Professor, Sport Business & Innovation and Director, Institute for Innovation & Entrepreneurship, Loughborough University, U.K.*

RESEARCH METHODOLOGIES FOR BUSINESS MANAGEMENT

Vanessa Ratten

Routledge
Taylor & Francis Group
LONDON AND NEW YORK

Designed cover image: Getty Images

First published 2023
by Routledge
4 Park Square, Milton Park, Abingdon, Oxon OX14 4RN

and by Routledge
605 Third Avenue, New York, NY 10158

Routledge is an imprint of the Taylor & Francis Group, an informa business

British Library Cataloguing-in-Publication Data
A catalogue record for this book is available from the British Library

Library of Congress Cataloging-in-Publication Data
Names: Ratten, Vanessa, author.
Title: Research methodologies for business management / Vanessa Ratten.
Description: 1 Edition. | New York, NY : Routledge, 2023. |
Includes bibliographical references and index. |
Identifiers: LCCN 2022040001 (print) | LCCN 2022040002 (ebook) |
ISBN 9781032323381 (hardback) | ISBN 9781032323374 (paperback) |
ISBN 9781003314516 (ebook)
Subjects: LCSH: Industrial management–Research. | Research–Methodology.
Classification: LCC HD30.4 .R38 2023 (print) |
LCC HD30.4 (ebook) | DDC 658.5/7–dc23/eng/20221026
LC record available at https://lccn.loc.gov/2022040001
LC ebook record available at https://lccn.loc.gov/2022040002

ISBN: 9781032323381 (hbk)
ISBN: 9781032323374 (pbk)
ISBN: 9781003314516 (ebk)

DOI: 10.4324/9781003314516

Typeset in Bembo
by Newgen Publishing UK

CONTENTS

TABLES

PREFACE

If you are interested in business research, this book is written for you. It helps you to learn about the research process and obtain best practice techniques. Thereby supporting you with information about how to design a good research study. Each chapter in the book focuses on a different part of the research process. This helps you to build your knowledge about research design. Along the way it provides best practice examples about how to do different types of research methodologies. This means it is pragmatic about the information needed by business management researchers.

This book is focused on understanding research methods specifically in a business management context. Therefore, it offers advice and suggestions to business management researchers about how to conduct an excellent research study. This includes providing examples of articles related to each topic together with specific activities designed to develop better capabilities in business management research.

All people interested in business management need to consider research methods. The way a study is conducted needs to be verified and discussed in detail. This will ensure readers trust the data and the explanations given for data collection. There are many different ways research studies can be conducted and this changes every year with a new technology entering the marketplace. As a result, information about research methods is continually evolving. The goal of this book is to include the most up-to-date and current information on business research methods.

Each chapter in the book follows a similar style in terms of it including an introduction, learning objectives, guidelines and conclusion. This enables the reader to feel comfortable that the material is being presented in a uniform format. Each chapter has a number of different headings that relate to the main topics that are being discussed. In addition, there are review questions, suggested activities and web exercises that enable the reader to test their knowledge on the chapter topic. At the end of each chapter are multiple choice questions that are useful in terms of testing core ideas and concepts discussed.

Included in all the chapters are discussion questions that make readers think about the topic of the chapter in a new way. The advantages and disadvantages of each topic are stated together with some exercises that are designed to be fun. At the end of each chapter are references as well as further reading suggestions.

I hope you will enjoy reading this book on research methods on business management. It is certainly an important topic and will play a key role in the development of your career whether it be as a researcher/scholar or researcher or someone with a general interest in research methods. It is important to think about how to conduct research and this book will help you learn the way to do this.

In conclusion, as research methods are crucial to the development of business management studies it is important that you read and do the exercises in each chapter. By doing so it will help you to reflect and think about the content. This will help increase your knowledge about the role research methods play in business management.

ACKNOWLEDGEMENTS

Thank you to Yongling Lam for her enthusiasm and support of this book project. It is very much appreciated. Thank you.

One of the first subjects I taught at the University of Queensland Business School was business research methods. I taught this subject for some time and enjoyed it as it was very relevant to business practice. During this time I read many articles and books on business research methods that were related to my interest generally in research methods. Therefore, some 20 years since I initially first taught this subject I am writing this book on research methods specifically for business management. It is important to focus on the business management aspects as the reasons for research differ based on the context. Thereby the methods and analysis techniques utilised in business management are context specific.

I dedicate this book to my mum Kaye Ratten for all the fun times we had. I have fond memories of staying in the Château Frontenac in Quebec city in Canada. I really enjoyed travelling with my mum and was lucky to travel to places including Memphis and New Orleans, which she loved. She was a fan of jazz music so enjoyed the atmosphere in both cities. We visited Beale Street and enjoyed listening to the music in the streets. I remember clearly her discovering musicians like Amy Winehouse in 2008 whilst living in Pittsburgh. She also loved listening and dancing to Jack Jones. When I was young, I have fond memories of her and my dad's records such as Sonny Terry and Brownie McGhee. This was back when we had a record player with records that is a bit different to the digital music that we have now. I also thank my dad David Ratten, brothers Hamish Ratten and Stuart Ratten, niece Sakura Ratten and sister-in-law Tomomi Ratten. Thank you.

1

ADVANCES IN BUSINESS MANAGEMENT RESEARCH METHODOLOGY

Introduction

This chapter discusses how research methodologies in business management have advanced over the years. This includes focusing on the current changes based on new thinking and technological innovation. A lot has changed in the past decade due to digital technology and data analytics influencing research methodology practices. Thus, this chapter provides a holistic overview of what the current state of development is regarding business management research methodology.

Learning objectives

- To understand advances in business management research methodology.
- To highlight recent changes in methodology practices.
- To examine future methodology practices.

What is research?

Research involves systematically reading and understanding information (Ammirato et al., 2022). This means adding to the current body of knowledge by understanding what has currently been done on the topic in the hope of advancing knowledge in the area. To do this, researchers obtain information and then test it through different kinds of methodologies. Researchers are those people who invest time and effort in discovering new knowledge. They are curious individuals who enjoy finding out new information (Cooper, 2015). This means they obtain previously unknown information in order to increase their intelligence. Research is important to the scientific discovery of new ideas and knowledge. How good research is defined is debatable due to the differing quality metrics available. Most agree that to be

DOI: 10.4324/9781003314516-1

considered as noteworthy research it needs to include some kind of new discovery. This means a new idea or technique comes to light based on the research findings.

Research quality is hard to assess as often it is based on a subjective assessment of one's work. This means there are inherent biases regarding how research is evaluated. Many journals rely on peer reviewers to assess research who may or may not be qualified. This is due to the peer reviewers research background and expertise not always being known. The actual process of doing research is difficult as there are many decisions to be made about what methodological approach should be used. This means research can be messy and complex due to the balancing act required in terms of weighing up different courses of action.

Lim et al. (2022) suggest that new research can take an applied or scholarly format. Applied research is mostly used to solve problems of a practical nature. This includes problems about organisational performance of managerial strategies. The idea behind applied research is that it is based on solving problems. For this reason, it often takes on an evaluative nature using current analysis techniques. This enables solutions to be developed based on current problems. Scholarly research is academic in nature and is based on advancing knowledge in a certain field of study. To be classified as scholarly research it needs to include relevant literature and connect with existing sources of knowledge. The main types of scholarly research are conceptual, empirical and review studies (Lim et al., 2022). Conceptual studies are based on ideas in terms of advancing new theories. They do not include any primary research and are based on assertions. When a new research field is being developed, conceptual studies are often utilised. Conceptual studies can include models to describe new occurrences. These models are then tested in other types of studies. Empirical studies contain new research and are based on the collection of data. This means they seek to test relationships between concepts. Review studies involve the discussion of a body of knowledge. This means trying to understand research gaps and the current state of the field.

OPENING DISCUSSION QUESTION

Why do you think research is important for business management?

Access to data

Researchers need to be able to access sufficient data sources in order to conduct a research project. This means considering whether an adequate sample can be obtained but also considering the collection costs. This means many researchers utilise databases that have existing information on companies. Commercial organisations often supply these databases for a fee in order for researchers to quickly access relevant samples. Professional and industry associations also sometimes have publicly available databases. However, in order to obtain an up-to-date and current pool of respondents, researchers might approach firms to ask them to participate in studies. It can be helpful to utilise industry contacts as a way of gaining trust amongst participants. In addition, local collaborators can help particularly if there are social or cultural differences.

Due to time and cost factors, secondary data is often used by researchers. This enables fast access to data that has already been collected. Instead of personally collecting data it can be easier to consult an existing data source. This is particularly relevant for research that requires large sample sizes and/or longitudinal information. Secondary data is classified as data that was not purposefully collected for a research study. This means it was gathered by someone else for a different reason. Secondary data can be used as a source of information to answer new research questions.

Sources of secondary data typically include government agencies and business associations. They may collect information on a frequent basis and provide access to others to analyse it. The data can be in a raw form or be in structured files. The data in a raw format often needs to be entered into computer programs in order to assess patterns. Structured forms of data normally are in files that can be easily analysed.

Mixed methods research

Mixed methods are an increasingly popular type of methodology. This is due to different types of data being utilised in order to derive findings. Mixed methods research is defined as "research that combines qualitative and quantitative data collection and data analysis within a single study" (Molina-Azorin et al., 2012:427). Often qualitative data in the form of interviews is combined with quantitative data in terms of a survey. This is due to both methods providing different sources of information.

The idea behind using mixed methods is that better data and more reliable information can be obtained by using different data-acquisition techniques. Mixed methods imply that a qualitative and quantitative approach is utilised but this is not always the case. Instead, two different types of qualitative or quantitative research techniques can be used. This does not normally occur as there is normally an emphasis on one type of qualitative or quantitative methodology. Therefore, it can be better to consider mixed methods as combining different research techniques or concepts. This means that mixed methods have four main perspectives: method, methodology, paradigm and practice (Creswell & Tashakkori, 2007). The method means using a certain technique like interviews, focus groups or ethnography. The methodology refers to quantitative or qualitative approaches. The paradigm means the philosophical underpinning of the study. The practice is how and why the data is collected. In order to understand mixed methods methodological approaches it can be helpful to focus on the advantages and disadvantages of business management research methodology. This is stated in Table 1.1.

TABLE 1.1 Advantages and disadvantages of business management research methodology

Advantages	*Disadvantages*
1. States the way research was collected.	1. Can be difficult to explain why the methodology approach was taken.
2. Provides information about the research process.	2. Time needs to be taken regarding detailing the methodology.
3. Enables others to read about the methodology.	3. Appropriate references need to be included.
4. Explains the reasons for the approach taken.	4. Can be difficult to write due to word counts
5. Provides a way to list related references to read.	5. May require new references to be added.

Research designs

In order to conduct a research study, the researcher needs to decide on a topic then derive a research question. There may then be research objectives that discuss sub-issues. After this has been done, the researcher needs to decide if they are conducting a qualitative, quantitative or mixed methods methodology. The main difference between quantitative and qualitative data is in the use of numbers. Quantitative data relies on numbers whilst qualitative data focuses on words.

There is a debate amongst researchers about whether qualitative or quantitative research techniques are better. This is largely derived from the academic background of the researcher in terms of the techniques they have learnt. In the social sciences particularly amongst sociology researchers, qualitative techniques are prioritised due to the belief they provide more detailed data. In the psychology and engineering fields, quantitative techniques are preferred due to an emphasis on numbers. Therefore, both qualitative and quantitative research each have their own advantages and disadvantages depending on the context.

Once the research design has been confirmed, exploratory research is normally conducted in order to test theories and refine theoretical frameworks. Exploratory research involves delving into new contexts that the researcher knows little about. This means new ideas and themes are being explored. Exploratory research is useful with innovations that have only recently been found, but there needs to be a focus on the validity of the research in order to evaluate if it is appropriate. Validity refers to whether the research methodology is reliable. It is an important way to determine whether inferences can be drawn from research findings. There are different types of validity but the main ones are internal, external, construct and statistical (Bouckenooghe et al., 2007). Internal validity refers to whether the research is measuring in the correct way the topic under investigation. External validity refers to how well a research study is measuring the concept in terms of the general environment. Construct validity refers to whether the construct items measure a topic in the right way. Statistical validity refers to whether the statistics found in the data are reliable indicators of the measures studied in the study.

ARTICLE READING ANALYSIS

Read the following article about the conceptualisation of research methodology among management academics.

- Saunders, M. N., & Bezzina, F. (2015). Reflections on conceptions of research methodology among management academics. *European Management Journal, 33*(5), 297–304.

Whilst reading the article think about why people conduct research in different methodological ways. As part of your thinking consider what the different academics in the survey reported in the article said about the nature of research. Consider what the different kinds of views were about qualitative, quantitative and mixed methods methodologies. This can include thinking about whether there is any right or wrong way to do research based on the use of qualitative and quantitative research techniques.

Innovation in research methods

Research methodology is constantly evolving based on the introduction of new techniques. This is the result of new thinking but also advances in technological innovation that enables researchers to obtain and analyse data in different ways. This means in order to publish research studies in high-impact journals and books, there is an emphasis on research methods innovation. Le and Schmid (2022:308) explain innovation in research methods as "the introduction and application of (parts of) research methods that are new or seldom used in a research field". Due to new technologies becoming available, research methodologies particularly in terms of data collection and analysis are changing. The idea behind innovation is that it introduces beneficial change. Innovation can generate new theories that expand a research field.

Innovation in research methods can include the use of non-traditional data sources such as nonverbal interaction that was not previously considered. This enables new research questions to emerge that can better solidify research findings. New data analysis techniques are also emerging that enable a more defined and interactive process to emerge. This helps in incorporating different sources of data that can help in triangulating research findings. Thereby adding to the way narratives and statistical analysis can be used in tandem in order to obtain unconventional results. Innovative methodologies often involve the use of different methodologies that have not been done before. This can include ways to collect data in terms of using new technology such as real-time information collected from geographical maps. Or alternatively new ways to present findings such as introducing a different kind of format.

In order to incorporate innovative research methods, the process should be transparent. Köhler (2016:401) defines transparency as "providing enough relevant information about the unfolding of the research (i.e. the research actions), so that the reader can gain a thorough understanding of it". This is increasingly important with many journals and books requiring researchers to add additional data sources so that the data can be used and tested by other researchers. By being transparent about data sources and analysis techniques, it helps research studies to be viewed as authentic.

Transparency in research requires clarity in a research context in terms of providing relevant information that is easy to understand (Köhler, 2016). This means including the reason or purpose for the study. To do this it can be useful to follow a consistent structure. Some researchers are being innovative by utilising different kinds of data-acquisition techniques. This includes obtaining information from people's experiences in terms of how their thoughts and perceptions change over time. Experience sampling methodology can be described as "detailed accounts of people's daily experiences over time and capture the ebb and flow of these experiences as they occur in situ (i.e. in the natural environment)" (Uy et al., 2010:33). This kind of innovative research methodology highlights how a person's responses can change over time based on environmental change.

As the environment constantly changes based on economic and social events, it helps for researchers to explain why the study requires attention means justifying its importance. This means highlighting recent events that have changed business conditions and require urgent attention. The researcher should connect the study to recent events to show its relevance. In addition, they should explain how the study fills a gap in the current literature.

The research should utilise established and verifiable methodological practices. This means explaining in detail what is being done and why. This can be done by utilising best practices. A logical step-by-step discussion of the method should be included. This will help to make the research process transparent and easy to explain. Some researchers are creative in what type of methodology they use. Supportive information should be included in order to explain the high quality of the data collected. This will enable others to feel comfortable that there is enough data to justify the findings. The researcher should explain how the analysis was refined.

The researcher needs to explain clearly what the data means by showing the linkages to theory and practice. This can be a difficult process particularly when new data is emerging. In order to be comfortable with what is being suggested, it can be helpful to include examples. Good analysis is needed in order to validate the findings. The researcher needs to go beyond just describing the findings and interpret their meanings. The results should be explained in terms of how they might affect other industries. This can be achieved by highlighting the theoretical and managerial implications of the study.

EXERCISE

Choose a local business in your area in which you could do research on. What kind of research approach would you use to collect data? What kind of resources are needed?

Large-scale research projects

Large-scale research projects are notoriously hard to manage due to the number of people involved in the project. Megaprojects are normally defined by the number of people involved and the monetary budget. They are important contributors to the global economy and enable issues to be systematically solved. Issues that affect society at large such as climate change and the ageing of the population can benefit from a coordinated approach. In the past, mapping of the human genome was done by an international team of researchers, so similar kinds of research projects are gaining traction. Whilst an international project has numerous benefits including the use of the 24-hour clock, it can also bring challenges in terms of different regulatory and institutional frameworks. These obstacles can be overcome but require a proper management strategy.

International projects can be difficult to coordinate due to operational requirements. This means whilst the sharing of knowledge is needed it can be hard to provide this information in an appropriate format to all those involved. This means the project should be managed in a transparent way in order to increase its value to society. Disputes over tasks can occur when there are unclear project guidelines. This gives rise to an inability to foresee the intended outcomes. In order to better manage large research projects, the following rules should be adhered to:

1. Assess the aim and relevance of the research project.
2. Consider each stage of the research process before embarking on the project.
3. Read widely before starting the research.
4. Evaluate whether different types of data collection methods might be needed.
5. Utilise the help of others in refining your ideas.

Methodological appendices

Methodological appendices can include any type of information relevant for the reported study. This includes a coding appendix where interview data has been coded. Methodological appendices are defined as "supplementary material that discusses how an author collected, generated, and analysed data" (Kapiszewski &

Karcher, 2021:287). This makes it easier for a person to insert notes in order to explain the methodology in more detail. By creating appendices it ensures that additional written information is stated about the methodology practices. This means people can read the information if they want that is relevant to specific stages of the methodology. It is in an appendix format as to provide further detail but makes it easy to read. This means it does not affect the general reading of a methodology section. The disadvantage of having appendices is that they can be time consuming to locate. This makes them useful additions but also increases their complexity. Often having additional information can assure others that there has been a greater attention to detail. Bleich and Pekkanen (2013) developed a formalised way to create a methodology appendix by suggesting it includes information about interview length and structure. This formalised approach was called an 'Interviews Method Appendix' and provides a useful way to present further interview information. This information is commonly asked for, but having a formalised structure to present it in can make it easier for the researcher.

EXERCISE

What are the main differences between qualitative and quantitative research? Which approach do you think is best and why?

Theory development

Theories are important in research as they enable ideas to be formulated into research propositions. This helps us understand what the data is saying and the reasons for this. The idea behind a theory is that it can be transferrable to other settings, thereby providing a way to understand the relationships between concepts. Gehman et al. (2018:291) states that theory "is a combination of constructs, relationships, between constructs, and the underlying logic linking those constructs that is focused on explaining some phenomenon in a general way". Theories enable people to express their views about what is occurring in society. This means that a theory is based on certain assumptions and logic.

A formal theory is a commonly used theory that is well established in the literature. Glaser and Strauss (1967:32) define a formal theory as a theory "developed for a formal, or conceptual, area of sociological inquiry, such as stigma, deviant behaviour, formal organization, socialization". This means it has normally been tested and refined over the years. Theories are often used as frameworks in order to explore a specific area of research. This enables each research article or book to build on previous work. By doing so the theoretical contribution is acknowledged and also evident in the research work. Corley and Gioia (2011:2) conceptualise theory as "a statement of concepts and their interrelationships that show how and/or why a phenomenon occurs". In some fields of research, for example, in information systems, theories such as the theory of planned behaviour and theory of reasoned action are well established and used as a theoretical framework for new studies. In addition, these theories are often combined to produce new theories or new components added due to technological developments. In the entrepreneurship field, the knowledge spillover theory of entrepreneurship is well established, but it bridges the knowledge management and entrepreneurship literature. This means new theories are increasingly bridging different bodies of literature in order to derive new ideas.

Grounded theory building involves a number of different steps that each take time to develop. In the initial stage a research question is developed in order to guide the research process. Normally grounded theory emerges from data in different ways. This includes information obtained from data that provides a narrative about what is occurring in the marketplace. This provides a sense of meaning about what the researcher thinks the data is suggesting, thereby it helps others to predict what might occur based on previous research. Most academic journals require a theoretical contribution that explains how the research in the article contributes to theory development. A theory can be hard to explain as there is a lack of consensus regarding its meaning.

Normally it is better to use a simple definition in order to explain a concept. Theories are often developed from other scientific disciplines then modified to suit new contexts (Suseno & Ratten, 2007). Corley and Gioia (2011) suggest that theoretical contributions can be evaluated based on their originality and utility. The originality refers to the newness of the research in terms of asserting new ideas. The originality can be incremental in terms of small advances to existing knowledge or revelatory in terms of making major advancements.

The utility can be viewed as being practically useful or scientifically useful. This means there are two main ways of evaluating the utility of a theoretical contribution. Practically useful means that managers can use the information in order to improve business practices. Managers may change how things are currently done because of the theory. Scientifically useful means that the theory can be incorporated into new research and development. Therefore, the theory is scientifically valued by other researchers.

The aim of a theory is to make sense of what is happening in the research world. This means the focus is on making assertions about why things occur in certain ways. Researchers generate theory based on their interpretations of data. A theory should help to explain why certain behaviour is expected. This means behaviour can be predicted in most cases by analysing previous behaviour. Not all behaviours will follow previous trends but most will.

In order to build theory, it helps to have a substantial body of knowledge in existence to support the assertions made. This means providing anecdotes or explanations about why things occur in certain ways. Shah and Corley (2006:1827) states that "grounded theory's distinctive features are its commitment to research and discovery through direct contact with the social world, coupled with a rejection of a priori theorizing". Therefore, grounded theory can be considered as a specific way to produce new theory. It enables novel theories to emerge based on data analysis. It is one of the most popular forms of theory development in the social sciences. The idea behind grounded theory is to obtain new understandings about relationships in society. This means emphasising patterns and interactions that occur over time.

There are different ways to conceptualise theory based on the views of the researcher. Substantive theory is developed for a specific purpose and highlights the need to explain different kinds of behaviour. Glaser and Strauss (1967:32) defines substantive theory as theory "that developed for a substantive, or empirical, area of sociological inquiry, such as patient care, race relations, professional education, delinquency or research organisations". The emphasis on substantive theory means developing a comprehensive understanding of a topic. By doing so, the theory developed will differ from existing notions of behaviour. In addition, it will have a richer explanation of how things occur in society. Many research fields prefer substantive theory as it provides a holistic way of understanding business developments. This is useful in explaining why things occur and predicting future events.

ARTICLE READING ANALYSIS

Read the following article about research methods in business that compares quantitative and qualitative analysis techniques.

- Lo, F. Y., Rey-Martí, A., & Botella-Carrubi, D. (2020). Research methods in business: Quantitative and qualitative comparative analysis. *Journal of Business Research, 115*, 221–224.

Consider why both types of approaches can be relevant in business management studies. Write down the main reasons why multiple research methodologies should be used in order to provide for better findings.

Credibility of scientific findings

In recent years, there has been an emphasis on replication studies to see if the findings of a study are the same in other contexts. There has generally been a poor replication rate in business studies due to the inability to produce the same results. Hensel (2021) suggests that the reasons for replication failure rates are mostly the use of questionable research practices. This has resulted in some journals emphasising the posting of supplemental data sources online. This provides a way for others to check and test the original data source. It also enables other researchers to use the data in new studies. The need for credibility in research findings has led to new initiatives and guidelines. This includes more transparency around each stage of the research project from initial research design to data collection and analysis. This is encouraging more openness regarding research practices.

In business journals there has only recently been an emphasis on including additional online data sources. This may be due to the ability of journals to store online data due to the use of cloud computing. It is also related to the way open innovation practices are emphasised more in society. Due to the many different research techniques used in business management studies, it can be hard to mandate commonly available information. This means there is some discretion as to what information is shared. In addition, there are privacy and security issues associated with the sharing of information.

The TOP standards were introduced as a way to provide research guidelines (Nosek et al., 2015). They now comprise eight standards (citation, data, code, materials, design, analysis, study preregistration analysis plan and registration replication) and two auxiliary evaluation items (registered reports and publication bias; Hensel, 2021). The citation standard refers to making sure prior research is properly cited in research. This is a standard practice, and there are software programs that enable researchers to efficiently do this. In addition, prior to publishing research articles, many journals and book publishers have an existing online system they can use to check references. This ensures citations are correct in research. There have been debates around citation practices particularly in terms of recognising previous research findings. The debate centres around who and why to cite research. The convention is that any direct previous research related to the topic is acknowledged in new research. This enables a history of research to be developed that adds to the scholarly discourse. Normally the citations are in a certain format depending on the journal or book preference. This ensures all published work is in the same style.

Data transparency refers to the data being available for others to view. In large data sets the data might be in an anonymous format so it is easier to share but in small data sets the information even though anonymised might still reveal participant information. This means there needs to be ethical considerations taken into account about the sharing of data. In some circumstances it can be justified, but in other contexts it would lead to negative outcomes. Thus, the advantages and disadvantages of data sharing need to be considered. This will ensure a more balanced approach to data dissemination. There can also be intellectual property considerations.

The coding used to analyse data should be available to others to scrutinise. This will lead to more transparency around the research process. This can include making available the materials used to do the analysis. The research design and analysis should be stated in a clear way that enables others to understand the way data was collected. This can include a study preregistration analysis plan that aims at stating what the research study is hoping to achieve and how it will do this. By registering the data it can then be replicated in other research contexts.

Guidelines

1. Think about what you want the research to achieve before finalising the methodology.
2. Collect as much information as possible about potential methodologies.
3. Look for good methodology books/articles/websites that might be useful for your research.
4. Compile a list of articles that can be on different topics to your topic but have a good methodology.
5. Try to acknowledge previous studies that used a similar methodology.

Developing expertise

In order to improve the quality of your research, try to read widely and if possible read one article a week in order to improve your knowledge of the area.

Pitch

Write a 2–3-minute pitch about why others should use a specific research methodology. In your pitch, please discuss the pros and cons of the approach and why it is most appropriate.

Checklist

1. There are many different research methodologies so do research first on which one is most appropriate.
2. Try to read widely about different kinds of research methodologies.
3. Keep a folder that includes useful articles on methodologies.
4. Try to include recent methodology references in your articles.
5. Think about how you can use mixed methods in your research.

Conclusion

This chapter has discussed the role of research methodologies in business management studies, thereby providing a holistic overview of why methodologies are important in any kind of research. There were many issues stated in the chapter that enable the reader to learn more about research methodologies. It is hoped that this chapter has provided you with the reasons why further reading is needed on advances in business management research methodology.

Review questions

1. Why is research methodology an important part of business management studies?
2. What is research and why is it important to current and future business practices?
3. What is the main difference between qualitative and quantitative research?

Suggested activities

Browse your local newspaper or website news channel for an issue you think is important. Write a plan for how you can collect data that helps provide more information about the problem.

Web exercise

Do a google search for the word 'research' and consider what types of articles show up. Change the search to include the words 'business management methodology' and reflect on the results.

Multiple choice questions

1. Research involves what kind of tasks?
    a. Systematically reading information
    b. Understanding information
    c. Adding to the current body of knowledge
    d. All of the above
2. What are the main types of scholarly research?
    a. Conceptual, empirical and review studies
    b. Conceptual studies
    c. Empirical studies
    d. None of the above
3. Secondary data can be classified as:
    a. Data that was purposefully collected for a research study
    b. Data that was not purposefully collected for a research study
    c. Both a and b
    d. None of the above
4. Mixed methods research involves
    a. Combining qualitative and quantitative data collection and analysis
    b. Just using one method
    c. Focusing on qualitative research
    d. None of the above

5. Internal validity refers to when research
   a. Measures the concept in terms of the general environment
   b. Measures the statistics
   c. Both a and b
   d. Measures in the correct way the topic under investigation

Answers: 1. D, 2. A, 3. B, 4. A, 5. D

References

Ammirato, S., Felicetti, A. M., Rogano, D., Linzalone, R., & Corvello, V. (2022). Digitalising the systematic literature review process: The MySLR platform. *Knowledge Management Research & Practice*, DOI:10.1080/14778238.2022.2041375

Bleich, E., & Pekkanen, R. (2013). How to report interview data. *Interview Research in Political Science, 1*, 84–105.

Bouckenooghe, D., Clercq, D. D., Willem, A., & Buelens, M. (2007). An assessment of validity in entrepreneurship research. *The Journal of Entrepreneurship, 16*(2), 147–171.

Cooper, H. (2015). *Research Synthesis and Meta-Analysis: A Step-by-Step Approach (Vol. 2)*. New York: Sage.

Corley, K. G., & Gioia, D. A. (2011). Building theory about theory building: What constitutes a theoretical contribution? *Academy of Management Review, 36*(1), 12–32.

Creswell, J. W., & Tashakkori, A. (2007). Differing perspectives on mixed methods research. *Journal of Mixed Methods Research, 1*(4), 303–308.

Gehman, J., Glaser, V. L., Eisenhardt, K. M., Gioia, D., Langley, A., & Corley, K. G. (2018). Finding theory–method fit: A comparison of three qualitative approaches to theory building. *Journal of Management Inquiry, 27*(3), 284–300.

Glaser, B. G., & Strauss, A. L. (1967). *The Discovery of Grounded Theory*. New York: Aldine.

Hensel, P. G. (2021). Reproducibility and replicability crisis: How management compares to psychology and economics – A systematic review of literature. *European Management Journal, 39*(5), 577–594.

Kapiszewski, D., & Karcher, S. (2021). Transparency in practice in qualitative research. *PS: Political Science & Politics, 54*(2), 285–291.

Köhler, T. (2016). From the editors: On writing up qualitative research in management learning and education. *Academy of Management Learning & Education, 15*(3), 400–418.

Lê, J. K., & Schmid, T. (2022). The practice of innovating research methods. *Organizational Research Methods, 25*(2), 308–336.

Lim, W. M., Kumar, S. & Ali, F. (2022). Advancing knowledge through literature reviews: 'what', 'why', and 'how' to contribute, *The Service Industries Journal*, DOI: 10.1080/02642069.2022.2047941

Molina-Azorín, J. F., López-Gamero, M. D., Pereira-Moliner, J., & Pertusa-Ortega, E. M. (2012). Mixed methods studies in entrepreneurship research: Applications and contributions. *Entrepreneurship & Regional Development, 24*(5–6), 425–456.

Nosek, B. A., Alter, G., Banks, G. C., Borsboom, D., Bowman, S. D., Breckler, S. J., … Yarkoni, T. (2015). Promoting an open research culture. *Science, 348*(6242), 1422–1425.

Shah, S. K., & Corley, K. G. (2006). Building better theory by bridging the quantitative–qualitative divide. *Journal of Management Studies, 43*(8), 1821–1835.

Suseno, Y., & Ratten, V. (2007). A theoretical framework of alliance performance: The role of trust, social capital and knowledge development. *Journal of Management & Organization, 13*(1), 4–23.

Uy, M. A., Foo, M. D., & Aguinis, H. (2010). Using experience sampling methodology to advance entrepreneurship theory and research. *Organizational Research Methods*, *13*(1), 31–54.

Further reading

Brennan, N. M. (2019). 100 research rules of the game: How to make your research world class; how to successfully publish in top international refereed journals. *Accounting, Auditing & Accountability Journal*, *32*(2), 691–706.

Cloutier, C., & Langley, A. (2020). What makes a process theoretical contribution? *Organization Theory*, *1*(1), 1–32.

Cornelissen, J. P. (2017). Preserving theoretical divergence in management research: Why the explanatory potential of quality research should be harnessed rather than suppressed. *Journal of Management Studies*, *54*(3), 368–383.

Cornelissen, J., Hollerer, M. A., & Seidl, D. (2021). What theory is and can be: Forms of theorizing in organizational scholarship. *Organization Theory*, *2*(3), 1–19.

Davies, M. A., Golob, U., Kernstock, J., & Powell, S. M. (2021). Journal of Brand Management: Editorial guidelines and expectations of authors. *Journal of Brand Management*, *28*(1), 1–7.

Delbridge, R., & Fiss, P. C. (2013). Editors' comments: Styles of theorizing and the social organization of knowledge. *Academy of Management Review*, *38*(3): 325–331.

Dyer, W. G., & Wilkins, A. L. (1991). Better stories, not better constructs, to generate better theory: A rejoinder to Eisenhardt. *Academy of Management Review*, *16*(3), 613–619.

2

LEVELS OF ANALYSIS IN BUSINESS MANAGEMENT RESEARCH

Introduction

The aim of this chapter is to provide information about why different levels of analysis are needed in business management research. This means focusing on the individual, group, team, regional, industry and country levels of analysis. Although there are also other levels of analysis that can be included in research discussions, these are the main levels of analysis used in business management research studies.

Learning objectives

- To understand why different levels of analysis are used in research by obtaining knowledge about how to write a research article.
- To highlight how individuals, teams and organisations can be analysed in research in order to understand why it is important to write in a concise and succinct way.
- To understand the use of multi-level analysis techniques in order to learn about how to be productive regarding writing up results.

Usage of different levels of analysis

In the business management field, it can be hard to integrate research that has been conducted at different levels of analysis. This is due to the business or firm level of analysis being the most popular form of analysis but often individual or group level of analysis being utilised. Aguinis et al. (2011:397) stated that "evidence of a divide between micro and macro domains is also reflected by the sometimes convergent research design, measurement and data analysis techniques used across these

DOI: 10.4324/9781003314516-2

domains". The micro-level research domain focuses on individual level behaviour in terms of behaviour and performance. This means many studies in the organisational behaviour area of management focus on the micro level. As a result, studies emphasise research methodologies designed to explore differences in behaviour between individuals. In human resource management, the micro level of analysis is preferred due to the emphasis on individual behaviour although there are also many studies conducted on groups and manager behaviour in a workplace setting.

Macro-level analysis tends to occur in the strategic management and entrepreneurship fields. This is due to the need to engage in economic issues affecting society. Often strategic management research is conducted in order to study patterns of behaviour. This enables predictions to be made about the likely directions of future industry growth. Moreover, in entrepreneurship studies the same emphasis on patterns is evident, but the shift in society is highlighted. By focusing on the policy implications, it can enable more detail to be obtained about practitioner relevance.

OPENING DISCUSSION QUESTION

Why do you think different units of analysis such as individuals, communities and regions should be used in research?

Self-awareness

Before starting any research project, an investigator needs to consider why they are doing research and what they hope to achieve. This will enable them to be aware of the goals and objectives of the research project. To do this in a proper way, the investigator should be clear about their own assumptions and preconceived notions related to the research. This will help to make the research project run in a more efficient way.

Every researcher has their own biases and experiences that shape the way they do research. To conduct ethical research, it is important to disclose anything that may impact the research process. This includes any potential conflicts of interest and ethical issues. Some of these issues may be evident before the research is started or emerge during the research. Deduction involves the process of proving something that has to happen in a certain way (Locke & Latham, 2020). This differs to induction whereby something is shown to actually occur in society. Another approach researchers can use is abduction, which suggests something is occurring in society. Abduction makes assumptions in terms of things most likely happening in a certain way.

When conducting any type of research study, it is possible that the researcher or participant may transfer some of their ideas to others. This means close attention needs to be paid to the process of transference. Winfield (2022:144) defines

TABLE 2.1 Advantages and disadvantages of analysis research

Advantages	*Disadvantages*
1. Enables different points of view to be considered.	1. Can be difficult to find different levels of analysis.
2. Allows for multiple interpretations of phenomena.	2. Can be hard to manage the data collection process.
3. Highlights the need to evaluate research in new ways.	3. Can be expensive to obtain different points of view.
4. Focuses on alternative ways of conducting research.	4. Some levels of analysis might not know about the phenomena under investigation.
5. Stresses the need to consider alternative points of view.	5. There can be both similarities and differences in opinion making it hard to obtain a consensus.

transference as "the process of the participant putting emotions on the investigation based on previous relationships in their lives". It is common that some kind of transference will occur between the researcher and the participant. The transference might be immediately evident in the response or in the interpretation of the research findings. Alternatively, it might take time to become evident. In research studies that are conducted over a long time period or in an intensive format, the transference may happen in a natural way. This is due to the rapport between the researcher and the participant. Although the researcher needs to be careful about any potential acquiesce bias in terms of the participant trying to respond in a way they think, the researcher will approve. Moreover, the use of leading questions should be limited as they can influence the results.

Countertransference is defined as "the investigator comes to put emotions on the participants based on prior experiences in their own lives" (Winfield, 2022:144). It is important to establish some kind of neutrality between the researcher and the participants. Otherwise transference can occur that results in the researcher interpreting answers based on their own experiences. This is not harmful but can determine how the findings are interpreted. This means attention needs to be placed on whether any kind of personal emotions is influencing the interpretation process. It is not possible to remove all kinds of transference due to emotional responses being part of individual behaviour. It is possible though to be aware of how stories can influence results. Transference is part of the reason why different kinds of analysis are needed in business management research. Table 2.1 states the advantages and disadvantages of analysis research.

Thematic analysis

Thematic analysis involves making sense of data by focusing on key themes. This is important in understanding the main issues that are emerging from the data.

There is not a specific way thematic analysis should be done, but there are common approaches as to how it is done. This enables researchers who use thematic analysis to be flexible in terms of how it is done. Thematic analysis is a practice-based approach in terms of the topics being derived from the analysis. This makes it an interpretative approach that allows for nuances to be acknowledged in research approaches.

Thematic analysis is a reputable and well-known analysis method. It enables a way to describe data and to acknowledge its meaning. In terms of coding data, a researcher should focus on both explicitly and implicitly stated ideas. This will enable concepts and experiences to be understood. The data coding can be done in an inductive way in terms of letting the content guide the analysis; or alternatively in a deductive way in terms of being driven by already understood concepts.

ARTICLE READING ANALYSIS

Read the following article about understanding research on values in business.

- Agle, B. R., & Caldwell, C. B. (1999). Understanding research on values in business: A level of analysis framework. *Business & Society, 38*(3), 326–387.

Whilst reading the article, list down the different points about how values are important in studying organisational phenomena. As part of your analysis, consider why values research based on different levels of analysis are important.

Writing a research proposal

Before conducting any type of research, it is useful to write a research proposal. This enables thoughts and ideas to be put into a written format so they can be recorded for later use. This helps in keeping track of what was proposed and actually completed regarding research work. It can take a lot of time to write a research proposal as each step of the process needs to be stated in detail.

A research proposal has many advantages in terms of it providing an overview of the research project. This enables the objectives and aims of the research to be identified. To write a good proposal, there needs to be sufficient explanation in each step. This includes the procedures to be followed as well as the timing of the research. This will enable others to evaluate the project in terms of its usefulness and relevance.

Martin and Fleming (2010) suggest that there are a number of steps for writing a research proposal. The main step involves summarising the information required in a research proposal. This involves providing a title for the research proposal. This is important as it is usually the first thing people read and it needs to get people's attention. This means it should use professional language that is used in the field of research in which it is written. For this reason, common phrases or terminologies can be used as it is assumed others in the field will know what the words mean. The title can also be thought-provoking or challenge traditional wisdom. Or alternatively it can be a title that succinctly explains the information contained in the proposal. The title should be the same in all documents related to the research proposal.

Types of research approaches

It is helpful to classify different research approaches according to the reasons why they occur. This enables categories and motivations to be applied to different kinds of research. Each research approach does not necessarily occur by itself as it can also involve the combination of different research approaches. Aityan (2022) suggests that the major research approaches are exploratory, descriptive, theoretical, experimental, simulation, analytical and creative. Each of these approaches will now be explained and examples will be provided in order to explain the approach in more detail.

EXERCISE

Choose one of your favourite movies and plan a research study that could be implemented to study the movie from different points of view.

Exploratory research

Exploratory research involves exploring a new idea to see if it holds true in practice. This means there is some hesitancy about what is known and unknown about a topic. The reason for doing exploratory research is to find out more information. This will help to understand the reasons for the problem. Many problems exist in society so exploratory research is needed in order to clarify the problem. This will enable the story or reason behind the problem to be identified. By doing so more knowledge can be obtained about why something occurred and how it can potentially be solved. Often businesses introduce new products into the market that are not successful. Exploratory research can be used to figure out the reasons for the failure. This will help to understand the mismatch and how better business decisions can be made.

Descriptive research

Descriptive research involves obtaining more detailed data about a phenomenon. This can include collecting statistics or other information that details how something occurs in society. The idea behind descriptive research is that specific information can be obtained. This can enable hypotheses or propositions to be tested and analysed. It can also allow information to be verified as a way of forecasting new demand. The emphasis of descriptive research is to enable data to be used for further analysis. This can include specific events and relationships to be analysed. Examples of descriptive research include finding out why, when and how consumers purchase something. This can include details about the size of products purchased and the frequency of the purchase. By conducting descriptive research, information about preferences can be obtained. This can be used in market research in order to make better future decisions. Businesses need to know why and how consumers purchase products in order to predict future sales. As each consumer is different but might have similar purchase intentions, descriptive data can be used to formulate new marketing strategies. By collecting information and then processing the data, a business can forecast future demands.

Theoretical research

Theoretical research includes developing ideas that can be used to explain events. This means coming up with new theories that can help to predict the way things will occur. This involves suggesting specific relationships between participants that result in an outcome. To do this involves setting parameters or processes in order to understand relationships. An example of theoretical research is suggesting that certain individuals with specific characteristics will likely behave in a certain way. The theory suggests something as likely to occur given the right kind of inputs. This helps in explaining why certain things occur based on environmental changes. Aityan (2022:15) defines a theory as "a set of statements or principles which are put together to explain certain facts, events, or phenomena and can be used for making predictions about those facts, events, or phenomena". This definition highlights how there are often certain patterns existing in a society that follow the same sequence. This means it is likely that things will occur in the same way based on previous trends.

EXERCISE

What is the difference between different levels of analysis in business management research?

Experimental research

Experimental research is generally defined as intentionally reproducing phenomena in a way to test relationships and interdependencies in the business environment. Normally experimental research is conducted in a controlled environment like a lab or office building setting. Experiments are useful in terms of understanding whether the same behaviour will occur. This means different types of experiments can be conducted in order to see if the result is the same. Experiments can be of a practical or applied nature depending on how they are conducted and provide a way of testing different stimuli in order to improve performance. This enables processes to be better understood and observed, thereby allowing for researchers to conduct experiments in controlled environments. By doing so, they can change different features of the experiment in order to improve satisfaction levels.

Simulation research

Simulation research involves simulating real-life contexts in a lab setting. This enables research to be conducted on phenomena in a cheaper and easier way. Often, it can be expensive to conduct research so simulations are used to understand the phenomena. Experiments can be conducted via computer programs that enable a phenomenon to be simulated. This enables events and processes to be studied as a way of mimicking the real world. As computer technology has advanced over the years, the capabilities of computer programs to produce simulations have increased. With the advent of big data and data analytics, the computer simulations have become more precise. The addition of artificial intelligence capabilities is predicted to further improve the calculation speed of simulations.

Analytical research

Analytical research involves critically examining material as a way of understanding what it contains. This helps in improving societies' knowledge about the topic. Being analytical can be difficult as it requires thought about the process. This means focusing on what is being done, why it has been done and the process to analyse the data, thereby making a more holistic approach to what the data means.

Creative research

Creative research involves any kind of study into innovative and new forms of research activity. This is important in progressing research in order to contribute to the existing body of knowledge. Creativity can be defined and conceptualised in numerous ways, but normally it refers to doing something differently, thereby incorporating new ideas and practices into research activity.

Theory-driven research

Theory-driven research focuses on using existing theory to explain the world (Schwarz & Stensaker, 2014). This means utilising theoretical frameworks in order to understand new contexts. Grounded theory occurs when informant's prior experience helps explain the current context (Gioia, 2021). This means the informant's understanding of what is occurring in the environment is linked to the theory. To do this the informant and theory-focused data can be combined in order to provide a better understanding of the relationships. Gioia (2021:23) states that "research needs to report first-order (informant-centred) and second-order (theory centred) data and findings", thereby, acting as a form of triangulation in terms of acquiring data from different sources in order to assess the findings.

Interpretive research can be explained as occurring when "research is grounded in informant interpretations (not mainly researcher interpretations of the structures and processes the informants themselves are using to socially construct the meaning of their experience" (Gioia, 2021:24). This means reporting closely what is actually being said without misrepresenting the data. This provides a more credible way to report research findings. It can help to look for explanatory theories that can explain informants' descriptions of their experiences. This provides deeper insights into what has occurred.

There is more emphasis on participatory and engaged research. This is due to the need to show impact and a connection with societal needs. This has resulted in more grants and funding going towards research that has a community connection. To do this a more long-term orientation towards collaboration with research partners is needed. This can lead to both academic and non-academic outcomes.

Some fields of business management such as international business have more of a history of relationally driven research practice. This is due to the topics covered in international business studies and the need to provide long-term results. Engaging in relational research practices can take time as there needs to be mutual trust. Interpersonal relationships are needed in relational research in order to assure participants about the joint goals. This means committing time and resources to the relationship.

There is more emphasis now on ethicised research practices. This ensures all parties have a say in how the research takes place. By doing so there are lower levels of power imbalances. This enables more egalitarian research practices to take place. Standpoint theory suggests that shared experiences of oppression enable more justified and contextualised results. This means collective understandings of injustice can lead to shared experiences, thereby enabling more information to be obtained about the experiences based on knowledge of power relations.

Many research relationships are temporal and based on a fixed time period. This means there can be less trust existing compared to more long-term research partnerships. Being involved in continued research engagement can mean more information is obtained. This means the normal time pressures associated with doing quick research might not apply. By moving more slowly and gradual in research partnerships it can enable more detailed knowledge to emerge. To do this research relationships need to be cultivated in order to produce results.

Participant-centred approach

In a participant-centred approach the respondent guides the conversation based on their emotional responses. By doing so they are telling their own story in a way they feel comfortable. To do this a researcher should not direct the conversation or show any kind of bias regarding the discussion. A researcher can help create a better research atmosphere by starting with an open question. This enables participants to speak freely and in a non-judgemental way. This means they can say what is on their mind without answering specific questions that require a yes or no answer. It helps to do this in order to encourage a more open discussion. This means being more collaborative in the research and asking participants for feedback.

Recognition of power dynamic and social location

In any kind of research there is a power dynamic that influences the relationship between researcher and participant. Usually there is no direct benefit to the participant from taking part in the research unless they are paid. This means the researcher is the one who obtains the benefit normally in the form of a research article. The researcher is normally in a higher socio-demographic strata that means they have a stable living situation. This may differ for participants who are dealing with other life issues.

A researcher normally holds a higher education qualification that means they have studied for a number of years. Moreover, they may be perceived as being more intelligent because of these qualifications. Therefore, this inequality needs to be considered in terms of the interaction that occurs between the researcher and the participant.

The identity of a researcher can be influenced by economic and social circumstances. This gives them situational power over respondents. This can be mitigated by having a researcher with similar ethnic or socio-demographic characteristics to the participant. Sometimes, this is not possible due to the subject matter. Researchers need to consider the moral implications of doing research. This is due to the topic or subject matter only relating to specific people.

In a positivist mode of inquiry, the variables and relationships can be measured. This is due to the purpose of the research being to predict causal linkages as a way of generalising the results to the general population. There are many ways to conduct positivist research, but normally it begins with a theory and hypothesis, thereby taking a deductive approach by reducing the data to numerical items. This means the researcher has a passive involvement in the research process and does not normally directly interact with participants. This results in having a more objective stance as to how the results are interpreted.

An interpretive mode of inquiry is more subjective as the research purpose is to provide an understanding of the context. This means an inductive rather than deductive approach is preferred. The variables in interpretivist research are difficult to measure so there can be hypotheses, but normally propositions are used. This helps in writing up the findings based on describing the context.

Choosing a field site

Choosing a field site to do research is part of the research process but can be difficult. This is due to the need to consider practicalities such as access and commitment. There can be gatekeeping obstacles in terms of getting a governing bodies acceptance to do research in a particular place. Some places might restrict the number of researchers in a site in order to reduce environmental damage. This means personal contacts can be helpful in identifying research sites. Once a place has been identified as being appropriate, there need to be negotiations with people in the area. This means approaching people who might take part in the research. Often a feasibility trip is conducted in order to assess the viability of the site.

Memory work

Memory work is an interpretive methodology that enables the researcher to be directly involved in the research process. This means it advocates for researchers to consider how they are involved in the design of research and the resulting knowledge obtained from the research results. In memory work, researchers interpret data based on lived experiences. This enables them to utilise their collective reflections as a way of understanding behaviour.

Knowledge is constructed in research through a subjective making process. Reflections about knowledge are created through the use of language. This means the knowledge of a researcher directly influences the research process. A researcher's interpretation is circumstantial and based on how they understand their experiences. This means findings and emotions are subjective and can be interpreted in different ways. The thoughts about these behaviours are based on the researchers' position in society.

A researcher influences how data is interpreted based on their thoughts. In memory work these thoughts are acknowledged as being an important part of the research process. This is due to the way they can provide insights into the social context. Researchers often feel certain types of emotions when conducting studies. This empathy can be directly observed and can influence research findings. It can be hard to be objective in research due to the direct interaction required.

More research is being conducted with participants. This contrasts to previous research studies that did not directly engage with participants. In some studies researchers pay for data that has already been obtained, thereby not directly experiencing its context. This means the data is analysed by computers or by individuals without regard to the context. This provides a sense of objectivity but may result in research that does not consider emotions or contextual factors.

Memory work involves obtaining knowledge through memories that is then codified and interpreted as a way to understand how participants feel about past experiences. This means analysing each memory as a way to understand the lived experiments of participants. Markula and Friend (2005:446) state that memory work "considers self a social product that arises from interactions with others, and the focus is to uncover the social constructions of experiences as they contribute to self-identity". Memory work is different to interviews as it relies on reflection rather than interpretation of interview transcripts. This means the emphasis is on memory in terms of thoughts rather than written texts. This enables the context to be understood rather than relying on written text. Often written words do not convey the tone or use of language that is important in understanding meanings.

In order to do memory work, it is necessary to have descriptive memories that provide detailed recollections. These descriptions should contain information that has not been altered. This means the information is stated verbatim without any kind of explanation. The recollections enable information to be obtained about the situation.

Memories provide a way of being in the situation. This enables researchers to explore how things occurred. This is part of the social construction process. Memories can be considered as the materials from which a person has made themselves (Markula & Friend, 2005). Crawford et al. (1992:39) describe memory work as tracing "the continuous process of the appropriation of the social and the becoming, the constructing, of the self". Onyx and Small (2001) suggest there are three phases in memory work: (1) writing the memories, (2) group discussion and analysis and (3) theorisation. Each of these phases contributes to the accumulation of knowledge, which helps to advance the research field.

Guidelines

1. Think about how a research study can be conducted using different points of view.
2. Consider who are the best people or entities to research regarding your topic.
3. Focus on the different ways people might perceive a phenomenon.
4. Highlight how it is important to consider new and previously unconsidered analysis levels.
5. Try to use multiple levels of analysis for the best results.

Developing expertise

Try to use alternative units of analysis in your research in order to acquire new knowledge.

Pitch

Develop a 3-minute pitch that explains why different units of analysis should be considered in research studies.

Checklist

1. Consider what the most appropriate unit of analysis is for your study.
2. Research previous studies that use the same unit of analysis.
3. Plan for how you will collect data.
4. Consider whether a multi-unit level of analysis study might yield better results.
5. Try to learn by reading or observing new units of analysis.

Conclusion

This chapter has highlighted how different levels of analysis can be utilised in business management research. This is important in advancing the research from the prevalent use of individuals or organisations in research studies to multiple points of view. The chapter provided an overview of different units of analysis such as the team, community and society level of analysis that can be used in future research studies.

Review questions

1. Why do you think different units of analysis should be used in research?
2. Do you think the individual or organisation unit of analysis is most appropriate or a combination of both?
3. How can different units of analysis be combined in research studies?

Suggested activities

Read two or three articles on a topic that you are familiar with and consider what unit of analysis they have utilised and the reasons for this approach.

Debate question

In pairs debate whether you agree or disagree with the idea that one particular unit of analysis is the best.

Web exercise

On the Internet do a search for 'units of analysis' in business management research and consider what the most popular results are.

Multiple choice questions

1. The micro-level research domain focuses mostly on
    a. Individual-level behaviour
    b. Group behaviour
    c. Society behaviour
    d. None of the above
2. Self-awareness is important in research due to
    a. External factors
    b. Biases and experiences shaping research
    c. Both a and b
    d. None of the above

3. Countertransference refers to a situation when
    a. An investigator puts emotions on the participants based on prior experiences
    b. Research topics are combined
    c. The study lacks external validity
    d. None of the above
4. Thematic analysis involves
    a. Doing statistical adjustments
    b. Analysing new theories
    c. Both a and b
    d. Making sense of data by focusing on key themes
5. Exploratory research is best defined as
    a. Doing research
    b. Testing a theory
    c. Exploring a new idea to see if it holds true in practice
    d. None of the above

Answers: 1. A, 2. B, 3. A, 4. D, 5. C.

References

Aguinis, H., Dalton, D. R., Bosco, F. A., Pierce, C. A., & Dalton, C. M. (2011). Meta-analytic choices and judgment calls: Implications for theory building and testing, obtained effect sizes, and scholarly impact. *Journal of Management, 37*(1), 5–38.

Aityan, S. K. (2022). Review of literature. In Sergey K. Aityan (Ed.) *Business Research Methodology*: 85–95. Cham: Springer.

Crawford, J., Kippax, S., Onyx, J., Gault, U., & Benton, P. (1992). *Emotion and Gender: Constructing Meaning from Memory*. New York: Sage.

Gioia, D. (2021). A systematic methodology for doing qualitative research. *The Journal of Applied Behavioral Science, 57*(1), 20–29.

Locke, E. A., & Latham, G. P. (2020). Building a theory by induction: The example of goal setting theory. *Organizational Psychology Review, 10*(3–4), 223–239.

Markula, P., & Friend, L. A. (2005). Remember when... memory-work as an interpretive methodology for sport management. *Journal of Sport Management, 19*(4), 442–463.

Martin, C. J. H., & Fleming, V. (2010). A 15-step model for writing a research proposal. *British Journal of Midwifery, 18*(12), 791–798.

Onyx, J., & Small, J. (2001). Memory-work: The method. *Qualitative Inquiry, 7*(6), 773–786.

Schwarz, G., & Stensaker, I. (2014). Time to take off the theoretical straightjacket and (re-) introduce phenomenon-driven research. *Journal of Applied Behavioral Science, 50*(4), 478–501.

Winfield, T. P. (2022). Vulnerable research: Competencies for trauma and justice-informed ethnography. *Journal of Contemporary Ethnography, 51*(2), 135–170.

Further reading

Aharoni, Y. (2011). Fifty years of case research in international business: The power of outliers and black swans. In R. Piekkari, & C. Welch (Eds.), *Rethinking the Case Study in International Business and Management Research*: 41–54. Cheltenham: Edward Elgar.

Barata, D. (2010). The extended case method. In A. J. Mills, G. Durepos, & E. Wiebe (Eds.), *Encyclopedia of Case Study Research*: 375–376. Thousand Oaks: Sage.

Burawoy, M. (1998). The extended case method. *Sociological Theory, 16*(1), 4–33.

Burawoy, M. (2009). *The Extended Case Method: Four Countries, Four Decades, Four Great Transformations*, and *One Theoretical Tradition*. Berkeley: University of California Press.

Easton, G. (2010). Critical realism in case study research. *Industrial Marketing Management, 39*(1), 118–128.

Fiss, P. C. (2009). Case studies and the configurational analysis of organizational phenomena. In D. Byrne, & C. C. Ragin (Eds.), *The Sage Handbook of Case-Based Methods*: 424–440. London: Sage.

Greene, J., Caracelli, V., & Graham, W. (1989). Toward a conceptual framework for mixed-method evaluation designs. *Educational Evaluation and Policy Analysis, 11*, 255–274.

Gummesson, E. (2017). *Case Theory in Business and Management*. London: Sage.

Harzing, A. W., Reiche, B. S., & Pudelko, M. (2013). Challenges in international survey research: A review with illustrations and suggested solutions for best practice. *European Journal of International Management*, 7(1), 112–134.

Hensel, P. G. (2021). Dissecting the tension of open science standards implementation in management and organization journals. *Accountability in Research*, 1–26.

Murray, R., Thow, M., Moore, S., & Murphy, M. (2008). The writing consultation: Developing academic writing practices. *Journal of Further and Higher Education, 32*(2), 119–128.

Ratten, V. (2021). COVID-19 and entrepreneurship: Future research directions. *Strategic Change, 30*(2), 91–98.

3

DESIGNING EFFECTIVE BUSINESS MANAGEMENT RESEARCH STUDIES

Introduction

Academic writing is different to other kinds of writing due to its scientific nature. This means it normally includes references to other articles written on a topic as a way of engaging with previous research. It can take time and effort to write in an academic way. This is due to the need to reference previous studies whilst discussing the current research project. Academic writing traditionally has been very formal. The increased usage of text messaging and abbreviations has changed this with more informal forms of language become popular. As a consequence, academic writing whilst still being very structured has become less restrictive. Hyland and Jiang (2017:40) state that in academic writing there has been "a gradual shift away from standard detached and impersonal styles of writing to ones that allow more personal comment, narration and stylistic variation". This change coincides with a more general interest in respecting one's individuality. Thus, in academic writing there is more acknowledgement regarding how people write in different ways. Furthermore, there are cultural and social issues regarding writing styles. This means academics are now expected to respect diversity. This leads to more personalisation regarding how people write in academic outlets.

Informality in academic writing can be hard to define due to different interpretations about its meaning. It generally refers to writing that has a more relaxed style. Language features such as the use of I or we can indicate informality. This is due to first-person pronouns not being used much in academia but being popular in everyday conversations. Hyland and Jiang (2017:41) state that "informality is generally hetero-defined, the Latin prefix meaning 'not, opposite of, without'". This means there are general standards associate with the use of informal language. This can be done in a deliberate way in order to make the writing more conversational or in an unplanned way when the writing is in the style of the author.

DOI: 10.4324/9781003314516-3

Society has a recognised set of practices regarding informal language. This is becoming more evident with text messaging that often uses abbreviations. Informal writing is normally considered more friendlier as it does not include big words that some people might not understand. Therefore, informal writing can be viewed as being more inclusive. This means it is based on current language conventions used by the general population.

Formal language denotes a person's position in society. Academics are people who have studied to obtain their degrees. This means they have learnt to use certain styles of language. This differentiates them from others who might focus more on easy forms of language. Therefore, academics by virtue of their studies tend to speak and write in a certain way. Academic language is characterised by its accuracy in terms of content and meaning. This is due to the need to provide accurate information. Normally this is based on calculations or references.

Informal writing can be perceived as casual and lacking in meaning. This means it is assumed people have not taken the time to speak or write in a proper way. In academia there is a need to be objective in terms of writing in a neutral way. Thus, personal feelings should not be evident in the writing style. Being objective is valued in academia due to the way it focuses on facts and not emotions. In academic writing, the message needs to be conveyed in the right way. This means including facts and statistics that support the assertions that are made. This is particularly important when the ideas conveyed are complex and difficult to explain.

OPENING DISCUSSION QUESTION

Why do you think it is important to design an effective business management research study?

Finding information

In order to do research, you need to find the right kind of information that fits your study. This means firstly obtaining most of the available material on the subject. With most journals now being published in an online format, it is easier to obtain access to them. If your computer is connected to your universities online system, you should easily be able to download and read articles. In order to search for articles, you may choose to use a database that helps you find relevant articles. By typing in a keyword, the articles related to this topic will be shown. If you want more specific articles, then you can refine the search by including additional words or time periods.

An article needs to have keywords that capture the meaning of the paper. As other researchers search for articles based on keywords, it is important to include the most appropriate ones. This will ensure your article is found by other researchers and consequently cited. The keywords should be linked to the title of

TABLE 3.1 Advantages and disadvantages of effective designs for business management research studies

Advantages	*Disadvantages*
1. Enables details about the study to be explained in a professional way.	1. Can be hard at the initial stage to know how the research will progress.
2. Highlights the thought process behind the study.	2. It can be time consuming to write down each step of the research process.
3. Enables each stage of the research process to be discussed.	3. Effective research studies require certain types of knowledge.
4. Focuses on the need to continually plan research studies.	4. The research study may change based on altering environmental conditions.
5. Allows for transparency in terms of research process.	5. Not all research studies will follow the same path.

the paper and the topic of the journal. The introduction of the paper presents the background information for why the research was conducted. Table 3.1 discusses in more detail the advantages and disadvantages of effective designs for business management studies.

Developing conceptual articles

In order to develop a conceptual article, it helps to focus on a new and emerging topic. This means it should not have been extensively published before or alternatively it provides a different way of looking at a topic. In the conceptual article it should be evident through a deep discussion about the relevance of the topic for readers. This can include recent advances in the literature that support the writing of a conceptual article. The uniqueness of the topic should be highlighted in terms of how it is filling a gap in the marketplace. A conceptual article should try to have some kind of theorizing within it that highlights new thought processes. This will help in acknowledging how the article is positioned relative to existing literature. Writing an academic article is complex as there is a need to position the paper within existing literature but also add to the discussion. This means a conversation regarding the literature is required. This includes fusing together different thoughts regarding a theory. Many business management fields are new and require additional theories. This helps to explain business-related phenomena but also recognises the existence of new market conditions such as that derived from the COVID-19 pandemic.

The essence of a good article is a clear and engaging writing style. This differentiates a well-written article from a poorly written article. An article should be based on existing literature and follow a logical structure. To do this, there needs to be multiple revision and feedback in order to improve the quality of the writing. The language and phrases used in an academic article should be clear and well defined. This means not using unnecessary jargon or complex language that others might find difficult to understand. The discussion should flow and there needs to be a connection between different parts of the article. This will ensure the article is written in a persuasive way that communicates the importance of the topic.

Barney (2018) suggests that the introduction section of a paper should include three main paragraphs. The first paragraph should briefly discuss what theoretical conversation the research is contributing to in the discussion. This means explaining the essential argument in the research study. The second paragraph should explain the reason for the study in terms of its significance. When writing an academic article, it helps to keep in mind that others might not be familiar with the topic. This means you should explain the research in a way that others will understand. This means telling a story about each step of the research process.

ARTICLE READING ANALYSIS

Read the following article about the use of sampling methods that discusses the gap between theory and practice that is important in academic writing.

- Sarstedt, M., Bengart, P., Shaltoni, A. M., & Lehmann, S. (2018). The use of sampling methods in advertising research: A gap between theory and practice. *International Journal of Advertising, 37*(4), 650–663.

Whilst reading the article, jot down ideas about suggested best practice for sampling procedures that can be implemented into academic writing. This includes information that is helpful in designing studies in terms of selection probabilities and sampling fluctuations.

Productivity in academic writing

Some people assume academics can write well but in reality only some can. This is due to the need to provide clarity in one's expression that can be easier done in a verbal rather than written format. Writing is a skill that takes time to refine and develop. In order to improve one's writing, it helps to practise on a frequent basis. This will enable the writing to be improved and lessons to be learnt.

Productive writers tend to spend a lot of time on their writing. In order to define a productive writer, there needs to be a comparison made with other researchers in their field. This will enable a judgement to be made on the number of outputs a writer has compared to others. Generally productive writers are enthusiastic and enjoy writing about their subject area of expertise. This means they are motivated to produce outputs that will have a societal impact. This normally involves writing on a frequent basis and persisting in times of hardship. Productive writers seize opportunities when they are found in order to advance a new idea.

Productivity is normally measured via the number of outputs a person produces. It can also be measured through the quality of contributions. In addition, productivity can be evaluated by whether the output is single or joint authorship. Publication outputs such as journals and books are normally more highly regarded than other kinds of outputs such as website articles. However, this is changing as academic evaluators respect new kinds of output that utilise technological innovation. This means blogs and social media posts are increasingly being considered as a component of academic research.

Citation data from the number of people who have referred to a specific written work can be useful to evaluate its influence on a research field. Journals and books have their own way to measure citations, and this can include using overall data downloads or data downloads from a recent three-year time period. Moreover, downloading figures that are often publicly available can help to assess the impact of an article.

There has been an increase generally in multiple-authored articles (Bahr & Zemon, 2000). This has been done due to the need to utilise specific skill sets that require joint collaboration. Thus, collaboration regarding publishing can be more efficient as tasks are shared. This enables people to specialise in their core strengths such as conducting a literature review or doing data analysis. As a result, the written output can be of a better quality overall. Recently journals have asked authors to state what tasks they have done in an article as a way of understanding what skills have been used. In addition, the percentage of overall contribution to the article normally should be stated in the footnotes of the journal article.

Academics face challenges in writing as it takes time and skill. Even though an academic can be extremely knowledgeable about a certain topic, to put this knowledge into a written format can be difficult. In order to be good and proficient at academic writing, practice is required. This means trying to write on a frequent basis and requesting feedback on your work. By continually trying to improve one's writing style, it can make a big difference to the quality of a scientific article. Good articles are direct and concise in their words.

The generally accepted way to write an article is to make it objective and impersonal. This means not including any kind of emotions that would reflect a form of bias. To do this can be difficult as the writer needs to write in a precise way. This means using the passive tense although increasingly there are more commentary articles being published that use the first person. Thus, writers should consult the journal or book as to writing conventions regarding the use of first or third person.

Good scientific writing utilises a range of references to support its assertions. This means including examples that provide evidence of why the discussion is relevant. The references should avoid any kind of bias that might not reflect the general statement. To do this means avoiding emotive language and statements about what is right or wrong.

Assumptions in the article need to be stated and clarified in terms of why they are being included. This can be done by attributing opinions to previously published work. Quotes are often used to do this as they provide a way of showing directly where a point of view comes from. This will help in building a discussion about differing views of a certain topic. The use of 'we' or 'our' is not generally used in academic writing. This is due to the need to focus on direct interpretations of scientific information. These plural pronouns are considered superfluous and digress from the scientific work being discussed.

Academic writing is considered as a being more difficult to read than other forms of writing. The use of references within the text makes it hard to read although with time these conventions and styles of writing other academics become accustomed to. The style of writing in academic journals is complex and is often used as a gauge of its quality. Although depending on the scientific field, the complexity of writing can differ. For example, in the humanities and social sciences there is an emphasis on words to describe behaviour but in engineering and technology management fields there is an emphasis on numbers. This means there can be many uses of technical words that only other academics would understand. This wording is expected in some academic fields and is a way to summarise research findings, thereby meaning that the academic writing in certain journals can be perceived as elitist as it excludes non-academics. In academic articles there can be jargon that makes the writing pretentious. This jargon can include abbreviations to long words. In addition, anecdotes or examples are included in academic articles as a way of providing more discussion around relevant points.

EXERCISE

Think about a business that has been affected by the COVID-19 pandemic. Write up a plan for how to ask questions about issues related to the COVID-19 pandemic.

References

Referencing is needed in academic work. Due to the availability of computer programs such as EndNote, it is easier to keep track of references. There are a number of different referencing styles depending on the topic. Normally researchers consult the key journal in their field as to what referencing style is preferred. Most referencing styles include the author surname, first name initials, year of publication, title of book, place of publication and publisher. For journals, the title of the journal, volume, issue and page numbers are included. Sometimes footnotes are also included as a way to comment on some particularly relevant issue.

References are needed in academic research in order to give credit to previous research. They also enable researchers to show the relevance of their work to previous studies. Thereby highlighting how they have added to the discussion. It is helpful to include references so others can read in more detail about a topic, thereby highlighting previous research but also showing respect for the work already conducted. Often researchers self-cite their previous work due to the need to acknowledge previous findings (Hellsten et al., 2007). This means self-citations can build a researcher's credibility in their field (Fowler & Aksnes, 2007).

ARTICLE READING ANALYSIS

Read the following article about using text for marketing insight.

- Berger, J., Humphreys, A., Ludwig, S., Moe, W. W., Netzer, O., & Schweidel, D. A. (2020). Uniting the tribes: Using text for marketing insight. *Journal of Marketing, 84*(1), 1–25.

Consider the reasons given for how researchers can use text data to generate insights. Think about the reasons given in the article for how the quality of the text produced influences the analysis process.

Peer review

In academia the process of peer review is important. It ensures the quality of an article is at a certain standard. For researchers, obtaining comments and feedback is important. Academic articles need to be written in a precise way. Typically, the passive rather than active tense is used. This means a range of views should be discussed in an article in order to stay objective. The goal of an article is to provide an overview of current knowledge on a topic and to suggest new ideas. This means trying to take a balanced approach in terms of what the current literature is suggesting. Normally personal opinions are not included in order to ensure the objectivity of the research. Academic writing is written in an authoritative way. This means there can be many usages of jargon or technical words only other academics would know.

EXERCISE

What is the difference between a good and not-so-good research design? What tips or advice would you provide to others in order to help them design better research studies?

The process of writing

The process of writing differs for each writer. Some people prefer to write directly into their computer via the keyboard. This is likely to be expected for those who grew up with computers and are considered digital natives. For older people, some still prefer paper and pens and then to transcribe their writing into the computer. Ramsden (1994:207) states that "research work only becomes 'a work' in the academic world when it takes on the conventional, physical form of a published paper or its equivalent". Academia is about producing new ideas through the sharing of knowledge. Research publications are central to academia as they provide a way to disseminate ideas. This can help speed up the process of learning and motivate others to do research. Academic reputation is closely tied to scholarly activities that include publishing research papers.

Kwiek (2016:380) states that research productivity is influenced by "the size of the department, disciplinary norms, reward and prestige systems and individual-level psychological constructs such as a desire for the intrinsic rewards of puzzle-solving". There are different reasons why some people like to do research and this can be considered based on necessity or opportunity reasons. Necessity reasons relate to the need to produce research due to being tied to monetary outputs. This means direct financial gain can be obtained from producing research. This is likely to be linked to grants or publication incentive systems. The time spent on academic training can have an influence on research productivity. This is due to the number of courses taken or mentorship that encouraged further scientific production. Moreover, a cooperative workplace climate can lead to more scientific outputs.

Productive researchers have the stamina to overcome obstacles and persist in their research. This persistence is needed when some journals require multiple rounds of revision. Moreover, the difficulty in finding a home for a research paper can be difficult when the topic or methodology is new. This means productive scholars have an inner drive that differentiates them from other scholars (Cole & Cole, 1973). This is evident in their enjoyment in doing scientific forms of research.

Guidelines

1. Think about what you want to achieve before designing the study.
2. Highlight the reasons for each stage of the research design.
3. Focus on analysing how each part of the research design leads to the next stage.
4. Explain how the research design fits with current practices.
5. Try to include references with your explanations.

Developing expertise

Try to update your online repository of research method articles on a weekly or monthly basis.

ARTICLE READING ANALYSIS

Read the article about qualitative research in marketing.

- Crick, J. M. (2021). Qualitative research in marketing: What can academics do better?. *Journal of Strategic Marketing, 29*(5), 390–429.

Consider whether there is now more qualitative research being published in top journals and the reasons for this increase. When reading the article, write down the mistakes that can occur when doing qualitative research and how they can be remedied.

Quality of scholarship

Wergin (2018) suggests that quality scholarship should be rigorous, credible and useful. Rigour means that the research has complied with quality standards. This means checking the research with previous sources of knowledge and amending it if necessary. Good-quality research takes time and each step of the process should be documented. This ensures standards are met. Researchers need to carefully choose their methods in a study in order to ensure they are appropriate. This includes the data collection tools and analysis procedures. As methodologies constantly change due to new technologies influencing the design process, researchers need to keep up to date with changes. This will ensure they are using the most relevant and innovative research approach.

Credibility refers to research being trustworthy. This means being transparent about how the research was conducted whilst respecting privacy concerns. It is important that the findings of a research study be in line with how the data was collected. This means ensuring it complies with norms practised in the field of study. To do this it can be helpful if the research findings suggest what the data says rather than providing definitive answers. This will ensure the data is plausible given the context.

Useful means that the research provides practical results. This can include adding to an existing body of knowledge in a way that has not been done before. Alternatively, it can involve giving suggestions to practitioners in order to improve their performance. This means that the results of a research study should yield some kind of benefit, thereby producing a valuable contribution to society.

In business management, researchers have tended to use data collected from one single time point. This convention means that many published studies use this approach. With the advent of social media and more real-time access to data this has changed. Now there are still data collected at one point in time, but increasingly it is also collected at other points in time and in different ways.

Researchers should be thoughtful about why they are using a specific methodology. It should be directed by their research questions and reason for doing the research. If possible, more episodic research based on certain events taking place should be conducted. This will enable more information to be obtained on how the context influences behaviour. There should also be immersive research in which the researcher is directly embedded in the context. This would mean greater insights could be obtained from responses but also via observations. Immersive research can help to obtain more information about unique behaviours over time. Business management researchers are characterised by their practical perspective regarding research findings. This makes them focused on the experience's businesses have in the global community. The underlying reason for doing business research is to make a difference in business.

Pitch

Develop a 2–3-minute talk about how you would design an effective business management research study. In your talk, discuss some tips you would give other researchers.

Different types of title

The title of a research output such as a book or journal article has an impact on whether others will read it. This means it is important to choose the right title that conveys the meaning of the work. Some researchers spend quite a bit of time in deciding on what the right title is. This involves researching other titles to make sure that their title has not been used before. Moreover, some researchers prefer a question in a title in terms of asking about a topic whilst others prefer short titles. There has been some research done on how more concise titles and simpler ones lead to more people reading the research item. Some considerations about how to choose a title are stated below:

1. General scientific types of titles

   These titles follow the same structure in terms of introducing the topic of the study. For example:
   - Social cognitive theory in technological innovations
   - Sport-based entrepreneurship practice and internationalisation trends

   Normally these kinds of titles focus on key themes or words designed to get the reader's attention.
2. Titles that include a cultural element

   These titles include a cultural element by referencing an event, movie or television show or other notable cultural item. They are designed to get readers' attention by mixing academic work with cultural events. For example
   - Should entrepreneurs persist or let it go? (Mentioning the song from the movie *Frozen*)

- Crisis management: The Gods must be crazy! (Mentioning the movie *The Gods Must Be Crazy* in the title)

3. Titles that use emotive language.

   These titles use emotions as a way of highlighting certain parts of the article. For example:
   - The fun of doing research
   - A happy and successful researcher

4. Titles using a question

   These titles use a question in order to produce an answer or debate. They highlight that at the moment the answer is unknown, but by reading the research an answer can be obtained. For example:
   - Is entrepreneurship a good thing?
   - Why should we research innovation?

5. Titles that provide a commentary

   These titles include the word commentary in order to show that they are a specific form of an article that provides an opinion. For example:
   - A commentary on sport entrepreneurship
   - A commentary about the future of artisan innovation

Structure of a research paper

Research papers are normally structured in a certain way that differentiates them from other kinds of papers. Normally they have a title, abstract, keywords, introduction, literature review, methodology, findings, discussion and conclusion. The length of each section will depend on what type of research is included in the paper and the conventions of the journal. For most journals, there is an emphasis on the literature review and findings section. This is due to the need for academic rigour in research papers.

A research paper has a systematic approach so that readers can compare different studies. This helps in ensuring consistency across research studies in ensuring a proforma is used. This makes it easy for the researcher to follow a logical sequence in terms of including certain types of information.

The title of the paper needs to convey the intended reason for the research study. Doing so in a succinct format can be difficult. Having an appropriate title is an important indicator of whether it will be read. Moreover, there have been suggestions that shorter titles can lead to more citations, which is relevant in establishing a researcher's profile. Thus, care needs to be taken in ensuring the title is both concise and relevant. It can be hard to think of a good title as there are many topics often discussed in a paper. Thus, the title should capture the attention of others in terms of wanting to know more. This means the title should be inspirational and exciting. There is some debates about what constitutes a good title with some people preferring short titles whilst others use commas and question marks.

The abstract of a paper should provide an overall summary of what the paper contains. This means including information about its purpose, methodology and main findings. The idea behind an abstract is that it can quickly be read in order to provide a short summary of the paper. As many people quickly glance at an abstract before reading a paper, it helps when it is written in an informative way. This means it includes enough relevant information for readers to want to know more.

In order to be a researcher it helps to enjoy the topic that you are researching. This means ideally you should choose a topic that you (not others) find interesting and this will be evident in your written work. When doing research, you should try to commit an open mind in terms of possibilities. This means the initial topic you have chosen to study might change depending on what you read. This will enable you not to be so transfixed on one area of study that you miss out on new opportunities. Moreover, when others make suggestions about related areas of research you should take their advice. This will enable you to delve into new areas of inquiry that can produce interesting outcomes.

As you progress with your research you should be discussing it with others in order to obtain feedback. This will enable new ideas to emerge and for existing ideas to be refined. It can help by presenting your research to others in order to hear their suggestions. Some people might criticise your research but you should be able to respond to their statements. This will help you to think about your research in different ways and to learn from the criticisms.

Checklist

1. Plan before doing a study about what you hope to achieve.
2. Read good studies that have a similar methodology to your study.
3. Think about the time and cost issues associated with your study.
4. Weigh up the advantages and disadvantages associated with different research methods.
5. Incorporate recent references to support your methodology.

Conclusion

This chapter has discussed how to design an effective business management study. To do this requires skill and effort involving finding the most appropriate method. Ways to explain a research study were stated, which include tips and suggestions for best practice procedures.

Review questions

1. How can research studies be designed in an effective way?
2. What is the difference between qualitative, quantitative and mixed methods research designs?
3. What kind of preparation and reading should you do before conducting a research study?

Suggested activity

Read three recent articles in a business management journal and consider what kind of trends there are in writing up research studies.

Web exercise

Go onto the Internet and type in the words 'COVID-19 business management research' in the search query. Read the topics that are found and think about whether the COVID-19 pandemic resulted in new research approaches.

Multiple choice questions

1. Academic writing is different to other types of writing because
   a. It normally includes references
   b. Has a scientific nature
   c. Engages with previous research
   d. All of the above
2. Informal writing can be best described as
   a. Casual
   b. Lacking in meaning
   c. Includes personal feelings
   d. All of the above
3. Productivity in academic writing is normally measured via
   a. The depth of writing
   b. The diversity of outputs
   c. The number of outputs a person produces
   d. None of the above
4. References should include
   a. The author name
   b. Year of publication
   c. Title of paper or book
   d. All of the above
5. Research productivity is influenced by
   a. Size of the department
   b. Disciplinary norms
   c. Reward systems
   d. All of the above

Answers: 1. D, 2. D, 3. C, 4. D, 5. D.

References

Bahr, A. H., & Zemon, M. (2000). Collaborative authorship in the journal literature: Perspectives for academic librarians who wish to publish. *College & Research Libraries*, *61*(5), 410–419.

Barney, J. (2018). Editor's comments: Positioning a theory paper for publication. *Academy of Management Review*, *43*(3), 345–348.

Cole, J. R., & Cole, S. (1973). *Social Stratification in Science*. Chicago: University of Chicago Press.

Fowler, J. H., & Aksnes, D. W. (2007). Does self-citation pay? *Scientometrics*, *72*(3), 427–447.

Hellsten, T., Lambiotte, R., Scharnhorst, A., & Ausloos, M. (2007). Self-citations, co-authorships and keywords: A new approach to scientists field mobility? *Scientometrics*, *72*(3), 469–486.

Hyland, K., & Jiang, F. K. (2017). Is academic writing becoming more informal? *English for Specific Purposes*, *45*, 40–51.

Kwiek, M. (2016). The European research elite: A cross-national study of highly productive academics in 11 countries. *Higher Education*, 71(3), 379–397.

Ramsden, P. (1994). Describing and explaining research productivity. *Higher Education*, *28*(2), 207–226.

Wergin, J. F. (2018). Finding the right design for EDI research. In A.E. Lize, Regine Bendl Booysen, and Judith K. Pringle (Eds.), *Handbook of Research Methods in Diversity Management, Equality and Inclusion at Work*: 36–59. Cheltenham, UK: Edward Elgar Publishing.

Further reading

Bouckenooghe, D., De Clercqm, D., Willem, A., & Buelens, M. (2007). An assessment of validity in entrepreneurship research. *The Journal of Entrepreneurship*, *16*(2), 147–171.

Creswell, J., & Tashakkori, A. (2007). Differing perspectives on mixed methods research. *Journal of Mixed Methods Research*, *1*, 303–308.

Crook, T., Shook, C., Morris, M., & Madden, T. (2010). Are we there yet? An assessment of research design and construct measurement practices in entrepreneurship research. *Organizational Research Methods*, *13*(1), 192–206.

Ferreira, J. J., Fernandes, C. I., & Ratten, V. (2017). Entrepreneurship, innovation and competitiveness: What is the connection? *International Journal of Business and Globalisation*, *18*(1), 73–95.

Jarratt, D. (1996). A comparison of two alternative interviewing techniques used within an integrated research design: A case study in outshopping using semi-structured and non-directed interviewing techniques. *Marketing Intelligence & Planning*, *14*(6): 6–15.

Lê, J. K., & Schmid, T. (2022). The practice of innovating research methods. *Organizational Research Methods*, *25*(2), 308–336.

4

QUALITATIVE BUSINESS MANAGEMENT RESEARCH METHODOLOGIES

Introduction

This chapter discusses the role of qualitative research in business management studies. The reasons for conducting qualitative research in the form of case studies and ethnography are examined. This enables an examination of how in-depth and detailed research can be obtained.

Learning objectives

- To understand the reason for conducting qualitative research
- To examine why a case study methodology can be used
- To highlight the benefits of using ethnographic data

Qualitative data

Reinecke et al. (2016:xv) state that

> qualitative methodology is a broad umbrella term for a diversity of data sources (e.g. interviews, textual and visual data, ethnography, and more recently netnography and video observation), ways to analyse them (e.g. grounded theory, discourse analysis, narrative analysis) and different epistemological/ontological commitments (e.g. realist, feminist, social constructivist, post structuralist).

Qualitative research involves the accumulation of large numbers of words. In order to manage these words it is useful to use relevant software packages. Quantitative

DOI: 10.4324/9781003314516-4

research uses assigned numeric values to precode answers. This means the analysis process is more straightforward than qualitative research that can be difficult to analyse. Qualitative data contains many different words so it is hard to translate this into numbers. Often qualitative researchers are the only ones who know and understand the data due to its contextual nature. This makes it hard for others to analyse without knowing the context. Increasingly qualitative researchers are being asked to include a quantitative data analysis component. Some qualitative researchers do not like to do this as they believe qualitative research is becoming too similar to quantitative research. Others think it is a good idea as it enables more rigour and transparency around the data analysis stage.

Qualitative methods can be used to build and test theory. Generally the emphasis is on establishing new theories based on the data obtained. This contrasts with quantitative methods that are generally used to test existing theories. Qualitative research has its origins in anthropology and sociology due to the emphasis on understanding lived experiences. This means a lot of the research in these fields was human-centred and interactive. This included ethnographic accounts that were derived from direct observations. In order to ensure qualitative research meets quality standards there has been an increase in mixed methods that use different methodologies.

Qualitative research is designed to elicit in-depth responses from participants. This enables more information to be obtained from participants. Therefore, it allows for credible as well as rigorous research when carried out in the right way. As it involves the researcher questioning and probing respondents, there are some suggestions that it is too subjective. This is a matter of perception as many qualitative researchers believe there is a science to their research just like quantitative research. Both qualitative and quantitative research have advantages and disadvantages, which means there is often a specific favoured methodology stance taken by a journal because of the views of the editor and reviewers. Some journals prefer qualitative research due to the way it provides comments about the participants' views and feelings, whilst other journals value quantitative data because it is numerically based.

Qualitative research is used to explain a phenomenon under investigation. This means the researcher asks questions and obtains answers, thereby enabling interpretative meanings to be explained. There is more human contact between the researcher and the participant in qualitative studies. This means that often a rapport is built that leads to further findings being discovered.

OPENING DISCUSSION QUESTION

Why do you think researchers should take a qualitative approach to data collection and analysis?

Reason for qualitative research

Qualitative research enables the researcher to be deeply immersed in the context. This helps them to explain the cultural and social conditions that are influencing the behaviour. In addition, depending on what is happening in the environment, the research design can be adapted and modified. This is helpful in adjusting studies to suit emerging conditions. In quantitative studies this might not be possible due to the need for a survey to be pre-planned based on existing measurement scales.

Qualitative research is better suited to new and emerging phenomenon. Reinecke et al. (2016) suggest that a qualitative researcher needs to focus on (1) describing why the study requires attention, (2) utilising rigorous methods, (3) including supportive information, (4) explaining what the data means, (5) conducting a good analysis and (6) explaining how the results can be generalised. This means there is not a full body of knowledge existing so the idea behind the use of qualitative methodologies is to obtain new information. In addition, whilst the data is being obtained further questions can be asked in order to explain the responses. This enables new theory to be developed. This contrasts with quantitative research that tests and refines existing theory. Normally in quantitative studies people have already developed and validated scales. This means there are existing measurement items available to test relationships between different concepts.

A researcher needs to feel comfortable in the methodology they choose. This is due to the need to know the science behind the methodology and to utilise the right tools. In addition, the methodology used needs to link with the studies objectives. Quantitative methods are often viewed as more sophisticated when in reality the same can be said of qualitative methods. This bias has meant qualitative research being marginalised and not respected as a scientific method. As a consequence, more emphasis is placed on positivist empirical methods that are used in quantitative research.

Qualitative research can be useful to understand the context behind a situation. This means incorporating situational elements such as place and time in the research. Qualitative research enables a detailed understanding of business practices. This includes why and how managers make decisions based on environmental conditions. The advantage of qualitative research is that more information can be obtained when asking interview questions. This contrasts with a quantitative survey in which the questions cannot be changed. It is appropriate to use qualitative methods when new theory is being built around a concept. Qualitative evidence enables new assertions to be developed and tested. A preliminary qualitative study is useful as a way to validate initial thoughts about a topic. This helps scholars to obtain information that can later be tested in alternative ways. This is helpful in generalising findings and making sure the results apply to different contexts.

Qualitative data can facilitate explanations that require a lengthy answer that cannot be done by a simple yes/no response. Qualitative researchers often feel a sense of empathy with respondents that is not apparent with quantitative research. This is due to the human contact occurring that means their values are sometimes

TABLE 4.1 Advantages and disadvantages of qualitative business management research methodologies

Advantages	*Disadvantages*
1. Enables information to be obtained directly from participants.	1. Can result in less objective data being obtained.
2. Allows for a more personalised approach to data collection.	2. Can be difficult to manage privacy concerns.
3. Highlights the need to gather more specific information from respondents.	3. Is time consuming in terms of obtaining relevant information.
4. Enables a focus on one key company or industry.	4. The data can change as new issues emerge.
5. Allows for a historical approach to be conducted around data collection.	5. Requires skill and expertise in the chosen research method.

evident in the research topics that are explored. Table 4.1 states the advantages and disadvantages of qualitative business management research methodologies.

Qualitative research philosophy

Qualitative methods are well suited to analyse complex phenomena as the issue can be explored in a detailed way. This means they can be used to generate new theories based on understanding environmental conditions in a different way. This enables researchers to elaborate and extend upon existing theories. The global business environment has changed rapidly in the past two years due to the COVID-19 pandemic. This has resulted in new challenges as well as changing business practices.

By implementing a qualitative methodology it can help in tracking the processes as they emerge. As quantitative studies rely on obtaining statistical data, that is based on achieving a sufficient sample size, qualitative methodologies can be used when data is hard to obtain. Reinecke et al. (2016:xiv) state that "qualitative researchers are uniquely placed to track novel phenomena in 'real time' as they occur". This is helpful when it is not clear why things are occurring the way they do. This enables events to be studied in a practical format. Qualitative research is conducted in an interpretative way that enables experiences to be analysed. This differs to quantitative research that is impersonal and relies on abstract concepts.

Positivism is often used in quantitative research due to the emphasis on surveys. Crick (2021:395) defines positivism as "an epistemological perspective, in which researchers believe that reality (the truth) can be accessed through scientific and objective tools". Qualitative research normally takes an interpretivist approach. This means interpreting information that is observable through interaction. This results in research methods that have a direct human element such as interviews being preferred that incorporate a critical realism philosophy. Crick (2021:395) states that critical realism involves "a philosophy, where researchers use multiple perspectives from their participants to challenge the assumptions of certain mainstream theories". This means having an open mind as to why and how things occur. Critical realists view research as a way to obtain different ideas about phenomenon under investigation. This means debating different views and taking into account alternative suggestions.

Qualitative researchers can use different philosophical stances in their research. The philosophy they choose needs to relate to what kind of research they are doing. This enables them to use critical realism, positivism or interpretivism based on their research situations. In qualitative research, the context is an important way to understand the findings (Welch et al., 2011). This is due to the context requiring knowledge only obtainable from certain people. Transparency is required in most forms of qualitative research in order to increase the trustworthiness of the findings. This means being open about how the data was collected and analysed. To do this means the researcher needs to be aware of the value of sharing knowledge. Whether this is possible can depend on the content of the data. Kapiszewski and Karcher (2021) suggest that to increase the transparency of qualitative research the following techniques can be used: preregistration, methodological appendices, annotation QA software output and data sharing. Each of these techniques will now be discussed.

Preregistration involves stating specifically the way data will be analysed before the data is collected. Given the exploratory nature of many qualitative studies it can be hard to do this. However, when it is done it allows each stage of the research process to be tracked. This enables the information to be timestamped so it can be referred to at later points of time. It also enables researchers to keep an account of when each piece of information was recorded. By implementing a preregistered method, it helps assure others that the interpretation is based on the available information. This makes the research more likely to be viewed as authentic but also scientific. Methodological appendices refer to additional information being included in the article that details the data collection and analysis process. Annotation QA software output refers to making comments on the output of any data analysis so that others can read the thought processes that went into the research results. Data sharing refers to giving information to others so that they have knowledge about what has occurred.

EXERCISE

Choose a business in your own area that has just started. Conduct secondary data analysis on why the business started and its focus market.

Qualitative data analysis

Qualitative data analysis is a key component of any research study as it enables the data to be interpreted in order to produce findings. The process of data analysis can be complex due to the need to code then verify results. This means it is typically a long process that can be time consuming. The use of computer programs can make the analysis stage less mysterious. This is due to the way computer programs offer audit trails in which others can see the steps undertaken in the analysis stage. This facilitates better data organisation and the retrieval of information.

Most computer-aided qualitative data analysis software have six main techniques: text retrieval, word frequencies, query by example, code frequency, code retrieval and coding co-occurrence (O'Kane et al., 2021). Text retrieval means a keyword or phrase can be searched for in a document. This facilitates an easy way to show the frequency of the word and thereby helping to understand where and why the word is occurring in the text. Once the words have been found they can then be inserted into tables or diagrams.

The ability to retrieve text is important in understanding the meaning of content but also enables coding to take place. This means emerging themes can be found in order to explore the main trends in the data. In the past, data was hand-coded and this took a long time to do. It also resulted in inadvertent errors that led to the misinterpretation of data. A computer program searches for words based on commands, thereby lowering the potential for error and miscoding. Sometimes people might have thoughts about what words are frequently being used in interviews, but a text analysis via a computer program can confirm this. When data is hand-coded, it can be interpreted in different ways. This is due to humans naturally systematically thinking about words in terms of their connections to other words. A computer program does what it is told to do and does not look for other words. This simplifies the data coding process.

Computer programs enable frequently occurring words to be found. This helps in identifying common words and supports the interpretation of data, thereby enabling a comparison between different texts in order to reflect on individual differences. A word frequency search can help researchers to engage in constant analysis. This enables more reflection to take place.

Researchers can utilise computer programs to query certain phrases. This enables text segments to be found that have similar meanings. This helps in understanding whether the text fits the theme of the phrase. When there is a large amount of text, it can be easier for a computer program to search text to review. This can be done through a process of experimentation in terms of cross checking the found items.

The Gioia methodology is a well-known way to interpret qualitative data (Gioia, 2021). Once the main themes or words have been coded, computer programs can help in assessing their frequency. This enables an assessment about whether the frequency of codes indicates a story. As there can be a long list of codes it can be helpful to search for the most important ones. This enables broad patterns to be found in the data, thereby assessing whether the frequencies indicate any associated emotions with the use of certain language.

After the coding process has been completed, coded text needs to be retrieved. This enables the codes to be checked and refined for their meaning. Codes with less frequency can be grouped with other codes or new codes found. This enables an assessment of coding co-occurrence to be completed, thereby indicating any closely connected codes in the text. There is more emphasis on longitudinal data in order to assess subtle changes over time.

> **ARTICLE READING ANALYSIS**
>
> Read the article about marketing analytics in research and practice.
>
> - Iacobucci, D., Petrescu, M., Krishen, A., & Bendixen, M. (2019). The state of marketing analytics in research and practice. *Journal of Marketing Analytics*, *7*(3), 152–181.
>
> Think about why more research is using social media as a source of data. Write down why big data and digitalisation have led to a change in the way data is accessed.

Qualitative data collection

In qualitative research, the right amount of data needs to be obtained before it can be analysed properly. This occurs when there has been a saturation of data. Saunders et al. (2018:1893) conceptualise saturation as "on the basis of the data that have been collected or analysed hitherto, further data collection and/or analysis are unnecessary". Saturation is a way for researchers to progress from the data collection to analysis stage. This means discontinuing data collection based on the belief that no new findings will emerge. The quality of the research findings is based on the assumption that data saturation has been reached. This means saturation is a way of showing the data obtained is the representation of the general population. This means the study has been conducted as a way of guaranteeing research excellence.

Saturation is achieved when the researcher sees the same kind of data being continually received. Glaser and Strauss (1967:61) define saturation as "no additional data are being found". This means there is a sense of similarity in the data and not much new data is emerging. Theoretical saturation is achieved when the data represents the suggestions stated in the theory. This means there is sufficient data to illustrate the theory. Starks and Trinidad (2007:1375) refer to theoretical saturation as "when the complete range of constructs that make up the theory is fully represented by the data". This means there is nothing new coming from the data that suggests alternative viewpoints and that this requires the emergence of no new themes. It can also involve the stopping of the analysis procedure based on the conclusion that all information has been received. The emphasis on the analysis being terminated rather than the data collection being stopped means there are different ways to define saturation. The analysis being the stage in which the saturation is reached means that this part of the research design is most important in ensuring a study is considered as valid. Within the analysis stage, the coding of the data might indicate saturation. Urquhart (2013:194) states that saturation involves "the point in coding when you find that no new codes occur in the data. There are mounting instances of the same codes, but no new ones". Thus, researchers should have protocols in place for measuring saturation in the coding stage of the data analysis.

EXERCISE

What is the difference between case study and ethnography research? Can both approaches be combined?

Case studies

Case study research involves interpreting data based on the environmental context. It involves multiple sources of information such as observation and interviews. It is highly descriptive in nature and is a powerful way to analyse a company. Case studies are often used to develop theory as they focus on why questions (Eisenhardt, 1989). This means information can be obtained based on a real-life context. In case study research, the unit of analysis is normally the firm, but it can be an event or region. Cases can be analysed using cross-sectional data from one point in time or longitudinal data collected at multiple time periods.

The four main methods to theorise from case studies are inductive theory building, natural experiment, interpretive sensemaking and contextualised explanation (Welch et al., 2011). Inductive theory building involves thinking about the data as a way to build ideas about what is happening in society. This means as new information emerges from the data a theory is developed. The context of the study provides a way of understanding what is being said. This means the theorising is about developing correlational effects. Natural experiment means that the data reveals specific indicators of behaviours that can be retested over time. Interpretive sensemaking refers to understanding data based on thoughts and feelings. Contextualised explanation means focusing on where and how the data was obtained in order to infer findings.

Often qualitative research is conducted in the form of a case study in order to understand a certain situation or context. Moghadam et al. (2021:2) state that "a case study is in-depth contextual analyses of one or a few instances of a natural phenomenon, such as a person, an organisation, a program, an event, a geographical location, or a decision". Case study research typically involves the use of both primary and secondary data. Primary data in the form of interviews and observations is supplemented by secondary data such as company reports and websites. Normally direct and indirect forms of observation are used in order to obtain a greater understanding of the case.

Case studies enable rich explanations and descriptions of phenomena to emerge. Sim et al. (2018) suggest the main ways to determine qualitative sample sizes are rule of thumb, conceptual models, numerical guidelines and statistical formulae. Rules of thumb refer to standards applied based on experience. This means the sample size is normally the same based on the field of study. Rules of thumb can also be based on the expectations of journals. Therefore, articles on a similar topic or theme may be referred to in order to understand expectations regarding the sample size. There are normally no clear rationale regarding what constitutes a good sample size. This means there can be some disagreements around what a right sample size means for a research study.

In conceptual models there is normally an associated framework that requires a certain sample size. Thus, the underlying reason for the study will be linked to the sample size required. If the study focuses on a specific topic, the sample size might be smaller. This will allow for detailed responses to be obtained from respondents. If the study is broad in scope, a larger sample size is required. This will enable the data to be generalised. In addition, if the data collection process is complex, a smaller sample might be used. This will enable information to be collected in an easier and more efficient way. Numerical guidelines refer to a specific number of cases being conducted that is considered as an adequate number of studies. Statistical formulae involves entering into a computer numbers about the cases in order to find out how many case studies should be conducted.

Malterud et al. (2016) suggest that a way to determine sample size is based on the information that is comprised in a sample. This is called information power and is influenced by the study's aim, specificity, background, dialogue and analysis (Sim et al., 2018). The aim for conducting a study can be based on the motivations of the researcher or the problem to be solved. This means the sample size is related to how the research is designed. The specificity relates to how easy or hard it is to obtain respondents. When the sample is based on general characteristics that many people have it can be easier to find respondents. If the sample requires participants to have unique characteristics, then it can be difficult to find respondents. The theoretical background refers to how developed the literature is regarding the study's topic. If the research topic has been studied in detail before the more likely there is already tested sample sizes. This means in new areas of research, the sample size needed might be larger in order to produce more generalisable results.

Case studies are used for their ability to understand the dynamics occurring within one setting. This means detailed knowledge can be obtained from studying the phenomenon in a single setting. De Massis and Kotlar (2014:16) define a case study as "a particular strategy for qualitative empirical research that allows an in-depth investigation of a contemporary phenomenon within its real-life context". This definition highlights that a case study is a strategic tool designed to obtain specific forms of information. To fully understand what is occurring a single setting enables an investigator to focus in depth on the behaviour.

The main types of case studies are exploratory, explanatory and descriptive (De Massis & Kotlar, 2014). An explanatory case study is utilised when there is a need to explain why something occurs in society. This means answering questions around how and why things occur. This enables the dynamics of the behaviour to be better understood in detail. It can be helpful to take an exploratory approach in order to refine existing knowledge and to increase the information valuable on the topic. This helps in building theory and enables different kinds of behaviour to be examined in more detail.

An explanatory case study focuses on explaining behaviour. This means asking questions about why something occurs the way it does. This means focusing on the why questions in order to open up our understanding of the phenomenon. Explanatory case study research involves gaining clarifications about behaviour in order to predict future trends. Rashid et al. (2019) suggest that the main phases of case study research are the foundation phase, prefield phase, field phase and reporting phase. The foundation phase means collecting information about the case in terms of available company reports and website information. The prefield phase means planning for the research that will be conducted. The field phase involves actually going into the business environment in order to obtain information. The reporting phase involves obtaining data and information that can then be analysed.

Case study research has been criticised for not being generalisable beyond the case studied. This is due to the way the case was analysed being based on impressions rather than facts. This is often not true as rigorous analysis techniques have been used. Generalisability can be defined as when research has "gathered broad enough evidence for an observed phenomenon to apply widely" (Gioia et al., 2021:21). This compares to transferability, which is defined as occurring when "even a single observation can represent a principle that applies to many different contexts" (Gioia, 2021:21). The difference between generalisability and transferability is based on semantics. It is a useful way to convey whether research findings have implications for other researchers. Focusing on transferable findings can offer a better way to understand whether the same results are likely to occur in other situations. This means the focus is on providing insightful explanations to contexts.

ARTICLE READING ANALYSIS

Read the following article about experimental research methodologies in organisational behaviour management and think about whether any kind of qualitative methods could be used as a supplementary source of information.

- Erath, T. G., Pellegrino, A. J., DiGennaro Reed, F. D., Ruby, S. A., Blackman, A. L., & Novak, M. D. (2021). Experimental research methodologies in organizational behavior management. *Journal of Organizational Behavior Management, 41*(2), 150–181.

Whilst reading the article think about why experiments as a research method result in unique findings. Think about how this research method differs to other kinds of research methodologies. Write down how experiments can be used in a laboratory and natural workplace setting.

Ethnography

Newth (2018: 684) describes ethnography as "a research output - a narrative driven expression of the researcher's fieldwork or as an assortment of data collection methods for the generation of rich insights into a particular social setting". Ethnography is an approach for doing research as it considers the context of behaviour. This means it focuses on the social setting in which the action is occurring. It emphasises the social setting and the linkages between other environmental factors. This includes observing the overall social context in which practices are conducted.

Ethnographic research provides a critical analysis of behaviour. By doing so the narrative or reason for the behaviour is emphasised. This includes thinking about why people do things based on the context, thereby stressing the role of interpretations based on cultural conditions. This means it can help to understand human actions and how they are embedded in the broader socio-cultural environment. There can be an unpredictability to ethnographic research in terms of not knowing how things are done. This means as it is a participative method the researcher has limited knowledge of the context. By immersing themselves directly in the context it can yield more in-depth and rich data.

Ethnographers glean information from their direct participation in the environment. This means that they personally experience the context and can report findings more accurately. The point of ethnographic research is to gain an appreciation of the environmental context. Ethnographers try to be credible in how and why they obtain certain sources of information. Newth (2018:688) defines credibility as "the degree to which the constructed realities of the study's participants are represented by those of the researcher". This means when conducting ethnographic research, the researcher needs to fully value the interactions that are taking place. This means focusing on the social dynamics and historical conditions. By doing so the researcher is a participant who can interpret behaviour. All researchers have some kind of bias because of their cultural and social conditions. This means different ethnographers might interpret things differently based on their own biases.

Ethnography provides a way to interpret data through a process approach. This means unlike quantitative research that takes a step-by-step approach with specific processes required, ethnography is more contextually based and reliant on environment responses. Ethnography requires both observation and participation. This means understanding how and why things are done based on the view of the participant. In ethnographic research the aim of data collection is to observe certain phenomena. This means the emphasis is on the researcher to watch and listen as to what is happening in the environment. This means being alert to changes and also considering inter-personal communication. In order to be observed, a researcher should be flexible in how they do this, thereby being able to adapt based on what the situation requires.

Normally ethnographic research is conducted in small settings. This makes it easier to observe different forms of behaviour. By doing so meanings can be attributed to different kinds of action. There is an emphasis in ethnography to study the natural environment in which behaviour occurs. This differs to laboratory and experiments where the environment is manipulated. Ethnography involves fieldwork as it focuses on real-time situations. This means the context for the research study is based on current conditions. The methods used in ethnographic research are flexible as they enable changes to occur over time. In order to identify field research as being ethnographic it should be studied in natural circumstances (Hammersley, 2018). This means there are no experimental conditions enforced by the researcher conducting the study.

Ethnography used to be a dominant research methodology used because of its ability to include descriptive data. Hammersley (2018:1) states "the term 'ethnography' has acquired a range of meanings, and comes in many different versions, these often reflecting sharply divergent orientations". With the advent of information technology, the use of ethnography has waned due to an increased interest in data analysis. Despite the increased Internet in technology-based research methods, ethnography is still popular.

Participant-centred approach

In some forms of ethnographic research, dealing with sensitive ethical issues care needs to be taken with research practices. This means considerations need to be given to issues related to power distances and inequality. Winfield (2022:143) states that "the six competencies for trauma and justice-informed ethnography include the following: (1) self-awareness, (b) participation-centred approach, (c) recognition of social location, (d) attention to trauma, (e) knowledge of professional limits, and (f) effective boundaries and self-care". Each of these competencies will now be discussed. Self-awareness refers to how well a person is observant about what is going on around them. This can include a participation-centred approach in which the researcher focuses on the participants' point of view from a first-person perspective. This means recognising the social location in terms of contextual ambiguities that may influence interactions. By doing so it can bring attention to the trauma faced by some people, but this can then bring about ethical and moral issues. Thus, the researcher needs to have knowledge of professional limits in terms of maintaining a duty of care. This can include instigating effective boundaries in terms of maintaining privacy in order to focus on self-care.

Ethnography involves utilising a triangulation of methods in order to obtain a better understanding of a real-life context. This means it is a form of writing culture in that the researcher is writing about what is occurring as it happens (Mitchell,

2007). In ethnographic studies a researcher has a personal engagement with the subject matter (Hammersley, 2018). This is due to the need to interact with the context in order to understand the social setting (Hobbs, 2006).

Ethnography is conducted in natural settings that enable real-life behaviour to be examined. This helps to understand how social activities occur based on group dynamics. To do this an interactive process is required in order to study behaviour in a systematic way. Hammersley (2018) suggests the main features of ethnography are that it is a long-term process, occurs in the natural environment and relies on engagement. Furthermore, he suggests it includes a range of data that documents what is happening based on the perceptions of the people involved. This means it seeks to understand in a holistic way what is occurring. There are various types of ethnography. Generally, ethnography refers to how the method is conducted and is understood by researchers. More specific forms of ethnography refer to ways the research is done such as through analysing web information or by using photographs. Thus, there is a great range of ways ethnography can occur and each has its own advantages and disadvantages. The diversity in methodological approaches is constantly changing based on new technology developments.

Netnography

Netnography is a popular research method due to its ability to capture feelings and sentiments from online interaction. Tavakoli and Wijesinghe (2019:48) state that netnography is "a qualitative approach to studying online communities through an ethnographic lens". Unlike ethnography in which the individuals are aware that they are being observed, netnography differs as it focuses on less obtrusive methods. This means it enables a way to understand how people behave in an online environment. Netnography enables online behaviour to be analysed that helps to predict patterns.

Netnography is a methodology that utilises the online environment. Netnography has also been referred to as ethnography for the Internet due to its usage of online information. This means it is a connective form of ethnography that relies on the digital environment. Researchers have also called netnography cyber or digital ethnography. This is due to the way it utilises computer-assisted knowledge that is available on the Internet.

Netnography is different to other types of ethnography due to the need for online information. This means it involves obtaining data from online sources that is then analysed. Netnography emerged in the 1990s when people started using the Internet. As the Internet has become more sophisticated and mobile computing has emerged, there are continually new ways of doing netnography. The increased usage of cloud computing means that more data is now stored in an online environment. This gives researchers access to large volumes of data.

Kozinets (2002:62) defined netnography as "a new qualitative research methodology that adopts ethnographic research techniques to the study of cultures and communities emerging through electronic networks". This definition was conceptualised in the early 2000s before the introduction of mobile computing and digital applications. Therefore, it focuses on electronic networks, which is a holistic term used to describe online activity. As the usage of the Internet rapidly increased in the 2000s, more detailed definitions of netnography have emerged in the literature. This includes De Valck et al. (2009:197) defining netnography as "a written account resulting from fieldwork studying the culture and communities that emerge from online, computer-mediated or internet-based communication". This definition encompasses technological innovation that individuals utilise on a frequent basis.

Netnography has adapted to new contexts based on changing environmental trends. Kozinets (2020:7) defined netnography as

> a set of general instructions relating to a specific way to conduct qualitative social media research using a combination of different research practices grouped into three distinct categories of data collection, data analysis, and data interpretation and their six overlapping stages or "movements".

This recent definition explicitly mentions social media, which is influencing how and when online data is collected.

Kozinets (2022) suggests that netnography involves four stages: (1) focus the research, (2) collect the data, (3) analyse and interpret the data and (4) communicate the research. In stage 1 the reason for the research is emphasised. This can include thinking about a research question that clarifies the reason for the study. Stage 2 involves collecting the data, which can mean obtaining information from different online sources. Once this is done stage 3 begins, which focuses on analysing and interpreting the data. This stage can take some time depending on the nature and quality of the data. Stage 4 involves communicating the research in terms of its main findings.

Kozinets (2020) suggests that the six movements of netnography are initiation, immersion, investigation, interaction, integration and incarnation. Each movement corresponds with a different stage in the data collection process. It helps to know each of these movements before embarking on any netnographic research. This will ensure the appropriate time is devoted to each step of the research process.

Guidelines

1. Do prior research on the case study prior to conducting primary data collection.
2. Think about what kind of qualitative data collection method is most appropriate.
3. Read relevant information related to the topic prior to the data collection stage.
4. Utilise a diary to record key dates and information related to your study.
5. Think about how future environmental changes might influence your results.

Pitch

Prepare a 2–3-minute presentation that details the reasons for conducting qualitative research.

Checklist

1. Think about which qualitative method is most appropriate for your study.
2. Prepare a research plan prior to collecting the data.
3. Consider how the data will be analysed.
4. Think about whether one or many participants are required in your study.
5. Consider the pros and cons of your qualitative methodology.

Conclusion

This chapter has discussed the reasons for conducting qualitative business management research. As part of the discussion the motivations for utilising case study and ethnographic research were stated. This enables a better understanding about the more direct and personalised form of data required from qualitative studies.

Review questions

1. Why do researchers prefer qualitative research to quantitative research?
2. What are the main reasons for conducting case study research?
3. How an ethnographic studies be planned over a long time period?

Suggested activity

Think about a business that is growing quickly and develop a case study about its success.

Web exercise

On the Internet search for information about case study methods and see what results can be obtained.

Multiple choice questions

1. Qualitative research includes
   a. Interviews
   b. Textual and visual data
   c. Ethnography and netnography
   d. All of the above

2. Positivism can be described as an epistemological perspective that focuses on
   a. Research is not possible
   b. Believing that the truth can be accessed through scientific tools
   c. Both a and b
   d. None of the above
3. Preregistration in qualitative research involves
   a. Applying for a patent
   b. Searching for new approaches
   c. Stating specifically the way data will be analysed before the data is collected
   d. None of the above
4. Computer-aided qualitative data analysis involves what kind of main techniques
   a. Text retrieval
   b. Word frequencies
   c. Code frequency
   d. All of the above
5. Saturation can be described as occurring when
   a. Further data collection and/or analysis is deemed unnecessary
   b. More data collection is required
   c. None of the above
   d. All of the above

Answers

1. D, 2. B, 3. C, 4. D, 5. A.

References

Crick, J. M. (2021). Qualitative research in marketing: What can academics do better? *Journal of Strategic Marketing*, *29*(5), 390–429.

De Massis, A., & Kotlar, J. (2014). The case study method in family business research: Guidelines for qualitative scholarship. *Journal of Family Business Strategy*, *5*(1), 15–29.

De Valck, K., Van Bruggen, G. H., & Wierenga, B. (2009). Virtual communities: A marketing perspective. Decision *Support Systems*, *47*(3), 185–203.

Eisenhardt, K. M. (1989). Building theories from case study research. *Academy of Management Review*, *14*(4), 532–550.

Gioia, D. (2021). A systematic methodology for doing qualitative research. *The Journal of Applied Behavioral Science*, *57*(1), 20–29.

Glaser, B. G., & Strauss, A. L. (1967). *The Discovery of Grounded Theory*. New York: Aldine.

Gorden, R. L. (1956). Dimensions of the depth interview. *American Journal of Sociology*, *62*(2), 158–164.

Hammersley, M. (2018). What is ethnography? Can it survive? Should it. *Ethnography and Education*, *13*(1): 1–17.

Hobbs, D. (2006). Ethnography, In Jupp, V. (Ed), *The Sage Dictionary of Social Research Methods*, 102–103. London: Sage.

Kapiszewski, D., & Karcher, S. (2021). Transparency in practice in qualitative research. *PS: Political Science & Politics*, *54*(2), 285–291.

Kozinets, R.V. (2002). The field behind the screen: Using netnography for marketing research in online communities. *Journal of marketing research*, *39*(1), 61–72.

Kozinets, R.V. (2020). E-tourism research, cultural understanding, and netnography. In: Xiang, Z., Fuchs, M., Gretzel, U., Höpken, W. (Eds), *Handbook of e-Tourism*, 1–16. Cham: Springer. https://doi.org/10.1007/978-3-030-05324-6_43-1.

Kozinets, R. V. (2022). Immersive netnography: A novel method for service experience research in virtual reality, augmented reality and metaverse contexts. *Journal of Service Management*, In Press.

Malterud, K., Siersma, V. D., & Guassora, A. D. (2016). Sample size in qualitative interview studies: Guided by information power. *Qualitative Health Research*, *26*(13), 1753–1760.

Mitchell, J. (2007). Ethnography, In Outhwaite, W. and Turner, S. (Ed)., *The Sage Handbook of Social Science Methodology*, 55–66. Los Angeles: Sage.

Newth, J. (2018). 'Hands-on' vs 'arm's Length' entrepreneurship research: Using ethnography to contextualize social innovation. *International Journal of Entrepreneurial Behavior & Research*, *24*(3), 683–696.

O'Kane, P., Smith, A., & Lerman, M. P. (2021). Building transparency and trustworthiness in inductive research through computer-aided qualitative data analysis software. *Organizational Research Methods*, *24*(1), 104–139.

Rashid, Y., Rashid, A., Warraich, M. A., Sabir, S. S., & Waseem, A. (2019). Case study method: A step-by-step guide for business researchers. *International Journal of Qualitative Methods*, *18*, 1609406919862424. https://doi.org/10.1177/1609406919862424

Reinecke, J., Arnold, D. G., & Palazzo, G. (2016). Qualitative methods in business ethics, corporate responsibility, and sustainability research. *Business Ethics Quarterly*, *26*(4), xiii–xxii.

Saunders, B., Sim, J., Kingstone, T., Baker, S., Waterfield, J., Bartlam, B., ... Jinks, C. (2018). Saturation in qualitative research: Exploring its conceptualization and operationalization. *Quality & Quantity*, *52*(4), 1893–1907.

Sim, J., Saunders, B., Waterfield, J., & Kingstone, T. (2018). Can sample size in qualitative research be determined a priori? *International Journal of Social Research Methodology*, *21*(5), 619–634.

Starks, H., & Trinidad, S. (2007). Choose your method: A comparison of phenomenology, discourse analysis, and grounded theory. *Qualitative Health Research*, *17*(10), 1372–1380.

Tavakoli, R., & Wijesinghe, S. N. (2019). The evolution of the web and netnography in tourism: A systematic review. *Tourism Management Perspectives*, *29*, 48–55.

Welch, C., Piekkari, R., Plakoyiannaki, E., & Paavilainen-Mäntymäki, E. (2011). Theorising from case studies: Towards a pluralist future for international business research. *Journal of International Business Studies*, *42*(5), 740–762.

Winfield, T. P. (2022). Vulnerable research: Competencies for trauma and justice-informed ethnography. *Journal of Contemporary Ethnography*, *51*(2), 135–170.

Further reading

Creswell, J. W. (1998). *Qualitative Inquiry and Research Design: Choosing among Five Traditions*, Thousand Oaks: Sage.

Lynn, N. & Lea, S. (2005). Through the looking glass: Considering the challenges visual methodologies raise for qualitative research. *Qualitative Research in Psychology*, *2*(3), 213–225.

Seidman, I. (1998). *Interviewing as Qualitative Research*. New York: Teachers College Press.

5

CONDUCTING INTERVIEWS AND FOCUS GROUPS

Introduction

This chapter discusses the role of interviews and focus groups in qualitative research. Interviews are one of the most popular tools for obtaining data. This is due to the way they enable interactive information to emerge. Focus groups will also be discussed in terms of how group interaction enables more detailed information to be obtained.

Learning objectives

- To analyse the reasons for conducting interviews as a data collection method.
- To highlight the benefits of interviews in terms of probing answers and obtaining additional information.
- To understand how and why focus groups are conducted.

> **OPENING DISCUSSION QUESTION**
>
> Why do you think interviewing is a popular data collection method?

Interviewing techniques

Interviews can be described as verbal or written exchanges between two or more people. They are conducted as a way to obtain and clarify information. Thereby they present a unique research tool to collect knowledge and find insights. Interviews are conducted because the researcher is unsure about how an interviewee will respond when asked certain questions. A researcher needs to be competent in interviewing

DOI: 10.4324/9781003314516-5

in order to do research properly, which ensures they use their knowledge and skills to conduct good research. Dilley (2000:133) states that "six questions are the heart of any interview: who, what, when, where, why and how". Who refers to the people who are going to be interviewed. The what refers to the topic of the interviews. The when is the timing of the interview and where is the location of the interview. Why refers to the reasons for the interview in terms of what data or information is being obtained and how refers to the way the interview will be conducted.

Interviews are a way to obtain information about an event or process. This means directly engaging with the person by asking them a number of questions. Interviews are useful in order to obtain information about experiences that can only be explained through verbal or written interaction. Most interviews are conducted in a verbal format due to the need to probe and respond to answers. This enables an interviewee to gauge the body language of the interviewee thereby helping to understand the meaning of their responses. Body language is an important way to understand non-verbal cues. The way a person describes something needs to be understood in conjunction with their body language. An interviewee can talk about their experiences as an individual or a member of a team or industry.

An interview generates mysterious overtones as the reason for it can be ambiguous (Gorden, 1956). This means it is sometimes considered as a manipulative research tool that can be used to obtain certain answers. Whether this is true is debatable as there are scientific methods to conducting an interview. Interviews can be conducted with multiple aims depending on the context. The primary aim should be to acquire information that helps to answer a research problem. Secondary aims can include to obtain information about a related issue. Thus, the success of an interview will be dependent on the motivation for conducting it.

In any interview a researcher needs to be aware of unconscious experience in terms of things happening in a non-verbal or contextual manner. Goren (1956:162) refers to unconscious experience as "behaviour which the respondent cannot report because he was not conscious of it at the time and not because of a fading memory, ego-threat, or the uniqueness of the experience". Gorden (1956) suggests that the three main types of unconscious behaviour are custom, circular reaction and active emotional stress in crisis. Custom refers to the ways things are done over time. This kind of behaviour is assumed in society. Circular reaction refers to how a person immediately responds to changes in the environment. Active emotional stress in crises refers to the heightened emotions felt in times of uncertainty.

The unconscious behaviour should also be examined from a time perspective in terms of chronological effects. Gorden (156:163) states that chronological aspect is conceptualised as "the relationship between the time an experience occurred and the time from which the respondent is actually or imaginatively viewing it". This will enable more information from the interview to be obtained about behaviour from a time and location perspective.

When conducting an interview, it is important to consider the time passed between the actual event and the time in which it is discussed. As time progresses, people might explain the event differently depending on how they recall the

TABLE 5.1 Advantages and disadvantages of conducting interviews

Advantages	*Disadvantages*
1. Enables the interviewer to ask additional questions.	1. May result in acquiescence bias.
2. Allows for answers to be explained in depth.	2. Can result in unanticipated findings.
3. Enables feedback to be incorporated into new questions.	3. Can be difficult to manage group interviews.
4. Encourages participation from respondents.	4. Requires consideration about the questions to be asked.
5. Allows for discussion to reveal new thoughts.	5. Requires the interviewer to manage time restrictions.

experience. Moreover, as the event is discussed in more detail recollections may get confused as others provide opinions over what happened. This means care needs to be taken regarding the use of imagination and other people's opinions of events. Interviewees can talk about an event in the present tense in order to recall vivid memories. This helps to discuss the event without any current distortions. Table 5.1 states the advantages and disadvantages related to conducting interviews.

Obtaining contextual information

Prior to an interview, the interviewer should try to obtain as much background information as they can on the interviewee and topic of discussion. This is a form of homework as the interviewer needs to research both the interviewee and topic. If possible previous interviews should be read in order to understand how the person might react to questions. This will help to make the interview more fluid in terms of asking and responding to questions.

Information about the cultural context should be consulted with prior to the interview. This means understanding how people discuss issues in their specific geographic region. Some cultures might be shy and reluctant to talk about certain issues. This means cultural comparison indexes can be used to understand whether the culture is individualistic or collectivist in nature. Moreover, there may be government restrictions about mentioning certain subjects that need to be considered. If the interview is conducted online, it may be easier than travelling to see the interviewee in person. However, it is likely more information can be obtained from direct face-to-face interaction.

The Global Entrepreneurship Monitor has information about entrepreneurial behaviour in different countries. Consulting with this data prior to conducting an interview can be helpful in understanding the cultural context. Prior to an interview being conducted the interviewee should try and gather information about the person. This can include information about their experiences. A google search of that person might provide useful information. Another option is to ask the person for a copy of their CV in order to read it before the interview. This can help establish a sense of solidarity or interest in that person. Thereby providing useful information that can be beneficial in the interview.

If a person has published articles or books it can be helpful to read their work prior to the interview. Or alternatively if they have some kind of special skill such as being a musician it can be useful to listen to their music. This will enable the interviewer to be knowledgeable about their expertise and to be considered a more sincere interviewer.

To obtain interview participants it can be useful to use snowball sampling. This means relying on referrals from others as a way to obtain new interviewee contact details. This approach is useful when a specific group of people with a common characteristic is required. Another way is to immerse oneself in the cultural context of the likely interviewee participants. This means attending educational, cultural or sporting events where the people sought for the interviews are likely to be in attendance. In an interview there needs to be some kind of mutual respect between the interviewer and interviewee. This means respecting different views and topic boundaries.

Once an interview has been conducted it needs to be analysed. This can be done by reflecting on the answers provided based on the context. Thereby considering how and why a participant answered questions in a certain way. This means an interviewer needs to listen carefully to what is being said based on the interviewees' body language. Sometimes information may not be verbally discussed but evident in body language. This includes certain emotions such as being happy or sad. In addition, the tone of voice or the emphasis on certain words may further explain the intended meaning.

The interview should be based on a pre-written protocol. This will help to make sure certain topics are discussed. However, the progression of the interview can change based on the responses. Certain questions may be emphasised in more detail or the answers can lead to new questions being asked. A good interviewer will have memorised the questions in the protocol so that they are not referring to a written document. In some cases, they may need to refer to talking points if there are a lot of questions. This will ensure the interview flows and does not lose momentum.

ARTICLE READING ANALYSIS

Read the following article about future research methodologies of lean manufacturing.

- Psomas, E. (2021). Future research methodologies of lean manufacturing: a systematic literature review. International Journal of Lean Six Sigma. https://doi.org/10.1108/IJLSS-06-2020-0082.

Whilst reading write down the different methodologies proposed about how they differ. Then classify each methodology in terms of its usefulness to your research.

The act of interviewing is a skill that takes time to master. This is due to some people being difficult to interview and finding it hard to verbally describe their thoughts. In addition, some topics are sensitive so how the interview is conducted is important. Interviews provide a way of obtaining information directly from the source. This means an interviewee can find out things that are not possible without talking to a person. An interview should be planned beforehand in order to make sure the appropriate questions are asked. An interview protocol can be used that acts as a guide or signpost for topics to be discussed.

EXERCISE

Choose a retail business in your area and draw up a list of questions to ask them about how they deal with the COVID-19 pandemic.

Open-ended questions

Open-ended questions enable participants to respond in their own way. This provides some leeway in terms of respondents being able to explain their responses. It means there is greater flexibility in the way people answer a question. This can make the answers more interesting but it can be hard to analyse the responses. Open-ended questions are structured but they are asked in order to obtain more information. There can be some prompting with the questions in terms of respondents being asked to recollect their experiences.

Open-ended questions can ask about general issues that do not require a specific answer. They can also ask respondents to evaluate issues thereby requiring them to provide some kind of detailed response. Evaluation questions seek a directive response in terms of requiring an answer in a certain way. Although how respondents answer is always personalised as some may talk more than others. Therefore, it is up to the interviewer to make respondents comfortable in order to allow them to speak in detail. This can be done with probing and asking for further information.

ARTICLE READING ANALYSIS

Read the article about participatory and deliberate methodologies.

- Saatcioglu, B., & Corus, C. (2019). Towards a macromarketing and consumer culture theory intersection: participatory and deliberative methodologies. *Journal of Macromarketing, 39*(1), 9–24.

Consider why action research is becoming more popular and how this changes data collection processes. Think about why action research takes a different approach to traditional forms of research. Write down how it includes cultural, historical, institutional, social and structural factors.

Interviewing through verbal histories

In an interview, the interviewee normally makes written observations that provide more insight into the answers. This enables notes to be made about what is observed in terms of body language at the time of response. There can be some inaccuracy from questionnaires as many people dislike paperwork. In addition, some concepts can be difficult to measure in a questionnaire. Often people are keen to share their experiences but prefer to discuss their experiences rather than responding to a questionnaire. In addition, in a questionnaire, the questions and answers are predetermined so there is not much room to express new ideas. This means the verbal history of a person can be conducted through an interview. This will enable a person to describe in detail their experiences.

Verbal histories as a data collection method have been around for a long time. This is due to the way information can be obtained through an oral discussion. Verbal history involves some kind of participant interaction with the person telling the story. In addition, it is easier often to verbally discuss things rather than putting the information in a written format. Verbal histories are a way of collecting valuable information. They are told in a narrative or storytelling way. This means events normally in chronological order are discussed.

The influence of researcher bias is decreased in verbal histories as they are listening rather than asking questions. This enables the person to tell their story in their own way at their own time. This enables a better comprehension about the events that have occurred over a certain time period. Once data has been obtained through verbal histories it can be a challenge to interpret. This is due to the volume of data and its unstructured format. Verbal histories are not anonymous, so care needs to be taken with its interpretation.

To conduct a verbal history interview it is necessary to provide a comfortable starting point. This will help in making the other person at ease. Normally a leading question such as can you tell me about your story is utilised to begin the interview. This kind of open-ended question makes it easier for the other person to respond in a way they feel comfortable. Once the interview has started then the other person should do most of the talking and there should be limited interruptions. This will enable the other person to speak at the pace they feel comfortable. Thereby not breaking the rhythm of the conversation.

EXERCISE

What is the difference between interviews and focus groups? Write down five advantages and disadvantages of each type of research methodology.

Group interviews

The assumption with interviews is that they are conducted between two people but often more than two people are involved. This can mean there are more than one person being interviewed at the same time. This often occurs due to time efficiencies. Group interviews can be difficult to conduct due to the need to obtain an equal amount of responses between each participant. One person might dominate a group and influence the answers of others. Therefore, there needs to be consideration of power differences in group interviews.

A group by definition means a number of interacting people. Groups can range in size from small to large numbers. Most references to groups imply that they normally contain between five to eight individuals. This generalisation means that the number of people included in an interview context is important in determining whether it is defined as a group interview.

There are numerous benefits to collecting information from a group. This is due to the direct feedback obtained from others in a group. In an interview that takes place between two people the interviewer normally leads the discussion. This means they take the initiative for asking new questions and obtaining clarification about answers. In a group the process of interaction differs as other group members interrupt and provide additional information. This means more information can be obtained at a quicker rate than is possible in an interview with only two people. Although care needs to be taken in a group interview that the views of everyone including those with differing opinions are heard. To do this can be difficult as some people might feel uncomfortable about interrupting the discussion. Thus, cultural and societal considerations need to be taken into account.

People in a group share a common interest. This means they have a sense of solidarity which influences the amount of information they share with each other. Miller (1995: 29) defines an interview as "a face-to-face situation in which participants have access to a range of each others communication skills, verbal and non-verbal". A researcher should have a repertoire of methods in order to provide a better result. This enables research to be explored in different ways in order to yield deeper insights. The advantage of interviews is that they provide spontaneity as they can lead to unexpected findings. This enables the possibility of finding different results to what was originally conceived.

An interview is a conversation between people for a purpose. The people involved can be strangers, friends or acquaintances. This means there is a range of different kinds of participants in an interview. Researchers should be aware of pre-existing relationships as they can influence the result of an interview.

An interviewer normally has more authority in an interview context as they are the person asking the questions. They organise the time and place in which the interview will occur. They initiate the contact and decide how long the interview will go for but sometimes the interviewee can influence this process as well. The topics for discussion are typically pre-planned but can change based on responses. An interview should flow smoothy but if it digresses to another topic it may take a different track. Whether this new information is useful will be based on the interviewer's perception of the information. If the usefulness of the information is becoming redundant then the interview may stop.

In an interview there can be status differences between the interviewer and interviewee. This is based on income level, age, gender as well as other factors. This means in order to decrease the role these factors play it is important to have a diverse interview team. This will enable a more contemporary and inclusive approach to interviewing.

Interviews have been perceived as being depersonalising as they do not take into account individual differences. This means they assume everyone is the same without considering personality and other individual characteristics. As a consequence, interviews have been criticised for being patronising and not being respectful. Interviewers are often scientists or other highly qualified people that may not be in the same socio-economic group as the interviewee. This means they can misinterpret information because they have not correctly identified its meaning. Thus, it can be helpful for interviewers to have some kind of familiarity with the people they are interviewing. This will help in deciphering non-verbal information as well as correctly giving the appropriate weight to different kinds of responses. Moreover, voice tones or pauses in a conversation may not be able to be recorded so need to be interpreted by an interviewer.

Interviews should be a pleasant occurrence if possible. This means asking appropriate and relevant questions whilst taking into account cultural differences. Being familiar with an interviewee can be useful but care needs to be taken that the answers are not preconceived notions of what is expected. Therefore, there should be some objectivity from the interviewer. This will help in having some kind of linguistic familiarity but also sensitivity.

Telephone interviews

Interviews can be conducted via telephone as a quick and easy way to connect with respondents. Telephone interviews can enable rapid responses to questions to be obtained although non-verbal information cannot be collected. Some people prefer to be interviewed on the telephone as they do not have to physically be seen by the interviewer. In time-sensitive situations it may be quicker to conduct telephone interviews. Then if necessary follow up with face-to-face interviews. A two-phased approach will enable more detailed information to be obtained.

In a telephone conversation there needs to be active participation in terms of verbal communication amongst the participants. Telephone interviews can be shorter in length due to the quickness in conversation. This enables questions to be asked in rapid succession. In telephone interviews, respondents can be asked prior to the conversation for an appropriate time to call. This will ensure they are ready to participate and informed consent is obtained. Alternatively, telephone interviews can be conducted on a random basis that provides for more spontaneity. This can help save travel time and make it more cost-effective.

People have different reasons for participating in interviews. Some view them as a way to fill time and decrease boredom whilst others consider them as a prestigious activity. Whatever the reason for participation, care needs to be taken as to how this will influence responses. There can be an acquiescence or willingness to please bias that means people will answer in certain ways. This means their responses may not be representative of their actual actions. Interviews can be viewed as a form of flattery whilst others see them as a privacy intrusion. The willingness of participants to be involved in interviews may be related to the topic of the interview. If it is about general issues related to the economy participation can be higher than if the interview is about a controversial topic.

Being assured of anonymity in responses can influence participation rates. This means people will answer questions when they can be assured that they do not have to identify themselves. Interviews will not uncover all information related to a topic but can help in identifying the most important elements. This enables multiple interpretations of a phenomena and enables a more holistic understanding of the topic. An interviewer should use paraphrasing to ensure responses are correctly recorded. In addition, prompts and reflections can be used in order to ensure an interview goes properly.

In a telephone interview there can be less distraction from external variables. This can mean the conversation is more intense and less prone to interruption. The cost of the telephone call can also be a factor in participation rates. In the past, telephone calls were expensive and timed but now with video calls they can be less costly and in many cases free. This has significantly affected the willingness of people to engage in telephone conversations. In interviews, the interviewer should record notes about responses. Doing this can be difficult due to the loss of attention.

Email interviews

Emails can be a source of interview data as they enable an efficient way to collect data and can provide immediate clarity due to the way written words are used for correspondence. The value of emails as a source of data is dependent on time and cost requirements. They offer a cheaper way to communicate with others as compared to phone and face-to-face interviews. By sending a list of questions for a person to respond to means that they can think about the answers in their own time and reply when ready. This has advantages in terms of obtaining more considered information but can lack the spontaneity of face-to-face interviews. Email interviews are often used in conjunction with other forms of interviewing techniques in order to supplement the information obtained. This helps the interviewer obtain a better sense of what is happening based on the environmental context.

Go-along interviews

Garcia et al. (2012:1395) describe go-along interviewing as "an innovative approach to obtaining contextualised perspectives by conducting mobile interviews in which the participant acts as a navigational guide of the real or virtual space in which he or she lives". A new interview technique that is contextually based and adaptive is called go-along interviewing. It enables changes to be made based on new events occurring. The interview takes an active role in the interview process and realises that they may need to change location in order to conduct the interviews.

In the past interviews normally were conducted in one location and it was generally a formal location such as an office. This meant the questions were prepared in advance and did not enable the interviewee much leeway in terms of asking additional new questions. This lack of flexibility meant there was a lot of interviewee acquiescence bias in terms of responding to questions in a way they thought was appropriate. If the interview had been conducted in another context the responses might have been different and allowed for more authentic replies.

Go-along interviews enable participants to co-create the interview and allows for a fairer way to conduct interviews. This contextualisation of experiences helps to readdress power imbalances and enables more information to emerge. The emphasis in a go-along interview is in exploring the context in real time. This immediacy offers a different way to obtain relevant information. It enables the interviewer to experience the context in order to obtain a more direct experience. Rather than having a sit down interview, a go-along interview means the interviewee can walk and talk at the same time. Thereby explaining responses in a different way based on environmental stimuli.

Go-along interviews capture the natural way people speak and behave in society. This means they are used as a way to collect contextual data that adds a layer of depth to the explanations. Traditional interviews are based on past events that can be difficult to recall. This means the recollections can change based on new experiences.

Some topics can be hard to discuss in a one-to-one interview format. This means go-along interviews are better suited to interview contexts based on sensitive material. A go-along format can be more conducive to interviewees who are reluctant to talk. By enabling collaborative and active participation it can be easier for interviewees to discuss their feelings. This helps create a sense of trust between the interviewer and interviewee. Thereby encouraging interviewees to be more frank and genuine with their responses. By doing so they are then open to additional questions. In a go-along interview the tension between interviewer and interviewee is relieved. This is due to the less informal nature and realisation that the interviewer wants to learn from the experience.

Focus groups

Focus groups involve a number of people coming together to discuss an issue. It enables people to speak about their feelings in a group setting. This enables new ideas to be formed that can help to solve a problem. To be classified as a focus group there needs to be the simultaneous involvement of a number of people. This usually means they sit together in a place to talk about a topic. Normally this occurs via face-to-face interaction in a physical format but can be done online. The idea behind focus groups is that the interaction of different people will enable ideas to be discussed in greater detail. Thereby facilitating insights that might not be evident from the involvement of just one person. People in a group can progress ideas based on previous suggestions.

To conduct a good focus group requires prior planning. This means thinking about what kind of people you require in order to obtain the intended results. The first step in conducting a focus group involves defining the problem that will be solved in the focus group. The emphasis is on solving a problem, but the focus groups might instead provide a number of suggestions or clarification about an issue. This means it is helpful to express a specific issue for discussion. The issue should be stated in a clear way that will enable concise answers to emerge from the discussion. There may be sub-issues that form part of the key issue. This means it can be useful to have one main issue than a number of sub-issues to discuss.

Once the problem has been expressed then the focus groups needs to be established. This means thinking about the appropriate number of people to include in the group. This depends on how easy or hard it is to recruit participants as well as the skills or knowledge they need to have. The time needed to complete the focus group should also be taken into account. This will help in understanding how quickly participants need to be recruited.

Participants in a focus group are selected in a purposeful way. This means selecting them based on their suitability for the study. Thereby enabling relevant people to be studied. Normally there is some kind of commonality amongst the participants of the focus group. This means they share a similar characteristic or behavioural trait. It can also involve similar socio-demographic features such as age or geographic location.

The number of participants chosen for a focus group may be restricted based on cost. If each member is being paid then only a certain number of people might be needed. If participation is voluntary it can be hard to obtain participants unless they have a desire to participate. The number of focus groups undertaken varies based on the complexity of the topic. An initial sample focus group might be conducted to test ideas. Once the questions are refined then further focus groups can take place. After each focus group the same or different questions can be asked. If similar questions are asked then this can enable more detailed data to emerge. If different questions are asked in each focus group, this might enable more broader perspective to emerge. Normally if the same questions are being asked, the researcher will keep holding focus groups until little new information is obtained. Normally this occurs after three to four focus groups but can differ based on the level of detail required.

It can be useful to have a protocol around the recruitment of participants. This will enable participants to be screened based on specific characteristics. This can include requiring a certain age group or area of expertise. Once participants are recruited they may need to sign a confidentiality or privacy agreement. This typically applies to topics about new product innovations that may still be under development. In addition, sensitive topics may need some discretion in terms of how they are discussed. Some topics such as religion may be contentious so care needs to be taken regarding which participants are sought for a study.

After the participants have been recruited it is then expected that they will behave in a professional manner. This means respecting other people's ideas and feelings about a topic. A moderator can be used to facilitate the progress of the focus group. This means probing interesting responses in order to delve deeper into certain issues. The moderator can also help solve disagreements between participants if they stop the progress of the focus group.

Some focus groups are self-selected as they rely on the participants to recruit other members. This can be helpful when specific personal characteristics are needed. This approach means that the participants might already know each other. When the topic under discussion requires specific types of people that are hard to find, having a snowball approach to recruitment can be helpful.

The number of participants in a focus group normally ranges from 6 to 8. This is generally accepted as the number of people required for a group discussion to be called a focus group. A group larger than ten people can be difficult to manage. This is due to some people not focusing on the discussion whilst others dominate the discussion. The ability of each person in a focus group to contribute to the discussion limits the number of people involved. It is important that people think that they can contribute and will have the time to voice discussions.

There is a trend towards small focus group sizes in order for each person to share their opinions. This means greater interaction can occur between participants. However, sometimes additional people may be sought in case some participants cannot attend. This ensures the optimal number of people are included in group discussions.

The length of a focus group is normally between 1 to 1.5 hours. This is a sufficient length of time in order for the topic to be introduced and the discussion to progress. Moreover, participants in a focus group might need some time to acclimatise. This ensures a sense of comfortableness emerges that allows rapport to be built between group members.

Guidelines

1. Think about why interviews might result in more detailed information.
2. Consider what questions to include in an interview.
3. Conduct prior research on potential questions to ask.
4. Think about whether individual or group interviews would be better.
5. Read articles and website information on interviewees prior to conducting the interviews.

Pitch

Develop a 2–3 minute talk about how to conduct individual and group interviews.

Checklist

1. Have an interview guide in place.
2. Try to ask the same questions to participants for consistency reasons.
3. Try not to deviate from the intended questions.
4. Consider how long the interview should go for.
5. Try to understand why and how participants answer questions.

Conclusion

This chapter has discussed why interviews and focus groups are useful data collection methods. The way to conduct interviews was stated in terms of time and resource allocations. Focus groups were discussed as an additional way to obtain information.

Review questions

1. Why do you think interviews are useful in research?
2. What different types of interviews can be conducted?
3. How many people should be in a focus group?

Web exercise

Go onto the Internet and type the word 'interview and group interview' into the search query and see what results are obtained.

Multiple choice questions

1. Verbal or written exchanges between two or more people can be called
   a. Focus groups
   b. Surveys
   c. Interviews
   d. None of the above
2. What are the six questions at the heart of any interview?
   a. For what, why, when, how come, length of time, for who
   b. Who, what, when, where, why and how
   c. None of the above
   d. All of the above
3. What kind of experience represents behaviour that cannot be reported because the person was not conscious of it at the time?
   a. Active
   b. Unrelated
   c. Conscious
   d. Unconscious
4. A person who asks questions in an interview is called the
   a. Interviewee
   b. Interviewer
   c. Both a and b
   d. None of the above
5. What types of questions involve asking for general information?
   a. Open ended
   b. Closed
   c. Discrete
   d. None of the above

Answers
1. C. 2. B., 3. D., 4. B, 5A.

References

Dilley, P. (2000). Conducting successful interviews: Tips for intrepid research. Theory into *Practice*, *39*(3), 131–137.

Garcia, C. M., Eisenberg, M. E., Frerich, E. A., Lechner, K. E., & Lust, K. (2012). Conducting go-along interviews to understand context and promote health. *Qualitative Health Research*, *22*(10), 1395–1403.

Gorden, R. L. (1956). Dimensions of the depth interview. *American Journal of Sociology*, *62*(2), 158–164.

Goren, A. L. (1956). Student activities and the teacher. *The Journal of Educational Sociology*, *29*(8), 351–352.

Miller, C. (1995). In-depth interviewing by telephone: Some practical considerations. *Evaluation & Research in Education*, *9*(1), 29–38.

Further reading

Aguinis, H., Ramani, R. S., & Cascio, W. F. (2020). Methodological practices in international business research: An after-action review of challenges and solutions. *Journal of International Business Studies, 51*(9), 1593–1608.

Cerar, J., Nell, P. C., & Reiche, B. S. (2021). The declining share of primary data and the neglect of the individual level in international business research. *Journal of International Business Studies, 52*(7), 1365–1374.

Goldman, A. E. (1962). The group depth interview. *Journal of Marketing, 26*(3), 61–68.

Granot, E., Brashear, T. G., & Motta, P. C. (2012). A structural guide to in-depth interviewing in business and industrial marketing research. *Journal of Business & Industrial Marketing, 27/7*, 547–553.

Li, H., Chen, Y. R., & Blader, S. L. (2016). Where is context? Advancing status research with a contextual value perspective. *Research in Organizational Behavior, 36*, 185–198.

Michailova, S. (2011). Contextualizing in international business research: Why do we need more of it and how can we be better at it? *Scandinavian Journal of Management, 27*(1), 129–139.

Patton, M. (1990). *Qualitative Evaluation and Research Methods* (2nd ed). Newbury Park: Sage.

Rapley, T. (2007). *Doing Conversation, Discourse and Document Analysis*. London: Sage.

Stake, R. (1995). *The Art of Case Study Research*. Thousand Oaks: Sage.

6

QUALITATIVE DATA ANALYSIS

Introduction

This chapter explores issues related to qualitative data analysis. This includes focusing on the reasons and rationale for the analysis process. As part of the discussion different qualitative techniques to analyse data will be discussed. This will help in building a holistic understanding about the way data can be analysed.

Learning objectives

1. To highlight the importance of analysing qualitative data.
2. To focus on acquiring knowledge about potential analysis techniques.
3. To examine in a step-by-step way how to analyse qualitative data.

> **OPENING DISCUSSION QUESTION**
>
> Why do you think data needs to be analysed in qualitative research?

Role of qualitative research

Qualitative research requires more direct engagement with participants so safety issues need to be considered. Kiyimba and O'Reilly (2016:92) state "in qualitative work the process and the content cannot be separated into discrete elements as they necessarily interact with one another". Qualitative research often requires a researcher to feel certain emotions or feelings. This is part of the research process

DOI: 10.4324/9781003314516-6

but can be emotionally overwhelming. In order to build rapport with participants, a researcher needs to understand their emotions. This can put the researcher's well-being at risk due to the amount of emotions they feel.

Researchers can feel emotions through direct interaction with participants, observation or by reading transcripts or other documents. In order to fully understand the participants' feelings, it may be necessary for a researcher to have some emotions. There is normally not much support given to emotionally demanding research as the researcher chooses to focus on this topic of interest. However, it is becoming more recognised in research studies and support is now given in many instances.

Emotionally demanding research is defined as "research that demands a tremendous amount of mental, emotional, or physical energy and potentially affects or depletes the researcher's health or well-being" (Kumar and Cavallaro, 2018:648). Kumar and Cavallaro (2018) suggest that there are four main types of emotionally demanding research topics: sensitive issues, personal trauma, traumatic experience and unexpected events. Research on sensitive issues include any topics that are hard to understand and often have unethical or moral dimensions. This can include sad events such as death or dying. It can include abuse and violence that is difficult to discuss. Personal trauma involves situations similar to what a researcher has experienced in their lifetime. This can include mental health issues that when discussed invoke unhappy memories. Traumatic life events refer to time periods that were sad and difficult to deal with. Unexpected events refer to sensitive topics or content that was not previously identified as being so.

Sensitive research is research that poses a threat to those involved. These threats can be known or unknown depending on the situation. Known threats often occur when the researcher knows that talking or reading about a topic will bring about certain emotional responses. Unknown threats occur by chance and can happen when the research touches on certain topics. Every individual deals with sensitive topics in their own way with some handling stress better than others. Moreover, people trained to deal with certain issues can be better prepared for the resulting emotional upheaval. They will still though feel some kind of emotional change when dealing with certain topics. Researchers dealing with sensitive issues can become too emotionally involved. This means they feel uneasy and a sense of sadness. Other emotions researchers can feel include psychological distress or a sense of hopelessness.

Emotions are part of qualitative data analysis as researchers need to consider what and why people are saying certain things. This enables them to build a sense of empathy for those involved and to consider their feelings. This helps bring a sense of rapport between the researcher and participants in any research process. Table 6.1 states the advantages and disadvantages of qualitative data analysis.

Research can be based on objective or subjective viewpoints. Objective research occurs when the knowledge is governed by relational norms. This means there are pre-existing ways to measure outputs based on suggested performance indicators. It

TABLE 6.1 Advantages and disadvantages of qualitative data analysis

Advantages	*Disadvantages*
1. Enables data to be compared across studies.	1. Can be difficult to analyse data due to knowledge needed in analysis techniques.
2. Enables more detailed information to be obtained.	2. Can result in data being analysed in a complex rather than simple manner.
3. Allows for inferences to be made from the data.	3. Can be expensive to obtain analysis software packages.
4. Allows for cross-comparisons to be made.	4. There can be debates regarding the most appropriate analysis technique.
5. Highlights that data needs to be analysed in order to provide results.	5. Can lead to time delays in publishing the research.

normally is characterised by statistical research that emphasises numbers. Subjective research is subject to interpretation and is based on individual experience.

Researchers have different beliefs about how and why research should be conducted. These beliefs can be considered as philosophical frameworks as they help guide research. Guba and Lincoln (1994) view these philosophies in terms of paradigms that include a researchers set of beliefs that influences their research. The main paradigms used in business management research are critical theory, interpretivism and positivism (Guba & Lincoln, 1994). In positivism the researcher believes that knowledge is guided by common sense. This means it is based on objective research designs with predetermined measurement scales. A positivist researcher remains objective and does not take a subjective stance. This ensures their independence and compliance with ethical standards. Positivists assume that phenomena can be understood in a scientific way. This means testing theories.

Critical theory studies seek to understand social systems as being inherently complex. This means focusing on how social relations are conducted based on power differences. Thereby acknowledging the role of inequality in society. Critical theory involves the thought that reality is based on history and is often reproduced in the same way. Thus, the context in which the research is conducted will influence how life is changing or staying the same. This means the focus is on critiquing society with the goal of making it more fair for all involved.

Interpretivism involves understanding behaviour based on the context. This means there are different ways of analysing the world depending on the beliefs of the researcher. Interpretive researchers acknowledge that the environment should be considered when explaining phenomena. This will help in analysing social networks and human interaction.

EXERCISE

Choose a topic that has been discussed recently in the media then think about the different ways to analyse interviews and other print media that discusses this topic.

Data analysis

In order to make sense of data Langley (1999) suggests seven strategies: narrative, quantification, alternative templates, grounded theory, visual mapping, temporal bracketing and synthetic. The narrative strategy involves constructing a story about the data. This means making suggestions about what the data says based on the context. To do this researchers need to have a realistic story that makes sense. This means making causal linkages between different themes evident in the data. This includes suggesting plausible answers to what data patterns mean. To do this requires describing the data in a way that others understand.

The variety of information contained in the data should be explained. This will help to convey how rich the data is and why it is important. Researchers need to interpret the data in a way that makes sense to others. This means communicating the usefulness of the data. To do this it can be helpful to focus on the authentication of the information. Moreover, it can be helpful to show how the data is valuable.

The quantification strategy focuses on analysing data through numbers and statistics. Langley (1999:697) states that

> in this approach researchers start with in-depth process data and then systematically list and code qualitative incidents according to predetermined characteristics, gradually reducing the complex mass of information to a set of quantitative time series that can be analysed using statistical methods.

This means that there is an emphasis on trying to find patterns in the data. This will help in understanding how different topics are perceived by respondents. By coding the data, it can enable researchers to analyse sequences of information thereby highlighting the way random or systematic information may emerge. The benefit of coding data is that descriptive patterns can be analysed. This means assuming the data is reliable and can be tested through rigorous means. Researchers can code data in different ways based on their methodological preferences. Normally dynamic simulation or event history analysis is done. This enables information to be obtained in order to assess causal feedback loops in the data.

The alternative templates strategy involves suggesting different interpretations based on a priori theory (Langley, 1999). This means finding different ways to analyse events based on theoretical suggestions. As it can be hard to find one theory that explains all the information multiple theories can be used. This can include multidisciplinary approaches that utilise different theories.

Grounded theory involves basing the analysis on existing theoretical frameworks. This means that the data is analysed in a way based on previous research findings. Visual mapping involves graphically depicting the data in a way in order to understand its meaning. Temporal bracketing is a way to deal with process data that is comprised of different time periods. A synthetic strategy involves relating different behavioural characteristics to the context or outcome.

ARTICLE READING ANALYSIS

Read the following article about the role of social research methodologies for social change.

- Tawodzera, M. C., Mabasa, L. T., & Themane, M. (2022). Contributions of Social Research Methodologies to Social Change: Giving Voice to the Voiceless. *International Journal of Qualitative Methods, 21*, 16094069211072417.

Think about how social research differs from other kinds of research and why it has increased in significance. Write down examples from the article that demonstrate the process of social change.

Coding data

After data has been collected it then needs to be coded. This enables assigning data to certain themes as a way of capturing the general content of the data. The idea of coding is to create links in the information. This means reading the data in either a dynamic or flexible way. Locke et al. (2022:264) describe the process of coding as "scrutinizing, pondering, and organising collected observations and relating them to theoretically relevant abstract features, possible relationships and research questions". Coding data in a dynamic way means there is some flexibility in associating meaning. This fluid approach enables new meanings to be ascribed to the data. Coding in a fixed way means having pre-determined themes. Thus, there is no definitive way to code data and it rather depends on the idiosyncrasies of the researcher.

Coding involves grouping data together based on ideas and observations (Saldaña, 2016). This means implying the data means something and can be classified in a certain way. To do this a form of bricolage can be used in order to analyse the data in a way that makes sense based on the research project. Methodological bricolage can be described as "the combining of analytic moves for the purpose of solving a problem, or problems tailored to one's own research project" (Pratt et al., 2022:211). It helps to take a bricolage approach in order to find a personalised and individualised way to analyse data.

Increasingly qualitative researchers are using methodological templates in order to explain the research process. This means the way qualitative research is conducted can be based on a formula. Pratt et al. (2022:212) define methodological templates as "standardized ways of conducting research that are used as formulas for shaping the methods themselves, especially data collection and analysis". This approach has been criticised for making qualitative research too much like quantitative research.

ARTICLE READING ANALYSIS

Read the article about international marketing research that discusses its current state and future trajectories.

- Leonidou, L. C., Katsikeas, C. S., Samiee, S., & Aykol, B. (2018). International marketing research: A state-of-the-art review and the way forward. *Advances in global marketing,* 3–33.

Consider how international marketing research has changed over time based on new methodologies.

Gioia methodology

In the first-order analysis stage of the Gioia methodology a large number of categories can result (Gioia, 2004). This is due to the large number of information being acquired from informants. Some researchers can feel overwhelmed at this stage due to the high level of detail required in terms of analysis. Some of the categories might not makes sense initially to researchers (Gioia & Chittipeddi, 1991). This means they need to contemplate what is being said and what it means (Gioia et al., 2013).

In order to reduce the number of categories the researcher needs to search for similarities in the data. This will enable a deeper analysis of the data to take place. Researchers need to think creatively when they do this as it can take time to reduce the number of codes (Gioia et al., 2010). It can be helpful to look at the data from different points of view. Trying to see the data in a new way can lead to different codes emerging. This can help in providing more clarity about the interview data. In the second-order stage of analysis new concepts should be emerging. This will help to build an understanding about what is currently lacking in the literature. Emergent themes that are relevant to existing theory should originate from the data.

After the first- and second-order themes have been finalised then the data structure can emerge. Gioia (2021:26) states that the data structure is "a way of understanding how all the terms, themes and dimensions relate to each other". This means it represents a way of capturing the key meanings associated with the raw data. To do this it helps to graphically represent the first- and second-order codes. By doing so it will ensure that all the data have been considered when proposing the overall structure of the data.

The data structure represents a static view of what has occurred rather than providing a changeable and real-time analysis. The data structure portrays what the researcher thinks the data suggests. This means showing the relationships amongst statements found in the data. The findings from the data structure should align with the data structure. This can be achieved by including direct quotes that represent the meanings of the codes. By showing explicit connections between the data structure and the responses it can provide better clarity about the results.

In qualitative research it is necessary to show how the data structure has emerged. This means linking the quotes in order to demonstrate data connections. This means suggesting plausible connects that are suggested by the available information. These connections should be revelatory in terms of providing a better understanding of what is occurring. This enables the data to systematically be analysed in order to discover new theories. In this way future analysis of text will be better recorded.

Manual content analysis

Manual content analysis generally undergoes nine different steps (Lee et al., 2022). Step 1 identifies the construct and topic to be analysed. Step 2 focuses on obtaining the complete texts that are then to be analysed. Step 3 focuses on the words or phrases to be analysed in order to understand the text. Step 4 assigns the categories of the content analysis. This includes providing example words or phrases to be searched. Step 5 involves generating a coding scheme for analysis. Step 6 involves a pretest or pilot test that is done on the coding scheme. Step 7 focuses on revising the coding scheme in order to increase its accuracy. Step 8 involves collecting the data to be examined then analysing its content. Step 9 focuses on providing reliability results of the content analysis.

Manual content analysis relies on human cognition around finding certain words. This means the people doing the analysis need to have a good comprehension of written words. Some information can be misinterpreted based on individual perceptions. This means some relevant information can be ignored. Computer-based analysis techniques can provide more objectivity around analysis techniques. This means they are programmed to search for specific words. However, computers cannot interpret idiosyncrasies in the data that humans can in analysis. Therefore, artificial intelligence combining computer and human knowledge can help in content analysis. Machine learning through artificial intelligence can provide a way to detect information and interpret it based on the context.

EXERCISE

What is the difference between different types of data analysis techniques?

Social listening analysis

Social listening is a way to obtain quick and reliable information about an issue. It can be used to identify trends and understand consumer behaviour. Instead of asking questions, social listening hears what others are saying. This is helpful in obtaining insights that would not be possible via direct questions. Westermann and Forthmann (2022:7) state that "social listening, social media analytics, social analytics and social media intelligence are often used as synonyms". Social listening is broader in scope than social media analytics as it does not just focus on media but rather general discourse. Thereby holistically analysing the way social information can be heard. Much of the information in social listening analysis is collected via the Internet. The use of big data has helped provide large quantities of information that can be analysed. There have been criticisms in the amount of data now available online as it can be hard to analyse. This means a deluge of data can undermine the quality of the analysis process.

Using drawings in research

Normally it is assumed that words are required for research but often drawings or pictures can be used. This is particularly useful in sensitive situations where drawings can have different kinds of meanings. Drawings can be used with words in order to depict responses. A participatory approach is used to facilitate meanings into drawings. Artistic expression is a way to empower those who are better at drawing than verbal communication.

A drawing can be analysed for the information it provides. This means it needs to be interpreted based on the context but also the situation of who drew it. Adults and children will likely draw differently so age differences should be considered. This will enable the story behind the drawing to be better understood.

Whilst a person draws they might also be able to describe what they are doing. This helps in gaining knowledge about the narrative of the story. Drawings can be made by individuals or in a group setting. When drawing with others it can help create a comfortable atmosphere. Observations can be made whilst a person draws. This helps to understand the emotions behind certain images.

Using photographs in research

Photographs can be used in research. This enables participants to take photos as a way to explain their story. Photos facilitate non-verbal information that can provide meaningful information. Giving people cameras can enable them to capture moments that they feel are relevant. This is a quicker way to capture a scene rather than having it verbally explained. It also provides a way to include different elements of the environment in one picture.

Photographs include content that others might view as irrelevant. Giving a person a camera to take pictures means transferring power to another. Thereby facilitating a process of trust between a participant and researcher. Asking a person to take photographs gives them more direction about the information they want documented to others. This means they need to make a choice about what kind of information to share. A photograph can be taken quickly but can be considered as a form of artwork. Photographs can be distorted in terms of altering the shape and picture. This means care needs to be taken in terms of considering the environment in which the picture was taken. This is due to people taking a photo choosing what to capture and at what angle. This means the photo is shaped by the person taking the picture.

Guidelines

1. Read previous studies about how they reported their methodology.
2. Try different types of analysis before finalising your analysis procedure.
3. Consider what kind of sample size is needed for the analysis.
4. Plan for the time needed to do the analysis.
5. Focus on the way data needs to be collected in order to be analysed.

Pitch

Develop a 2–3 minute talk about why qualitative data should be analysed. Discuss the different main analysis techniques.

Checklist

1. Decide on what analysis technique to use before collecting data.
2. Read articles about analysis techniques.
3. Highlight the main findings from the analysis.
4. Utilise good examples of methodology sections of articles.
5. Try to stay ahead with methodology analysis developments.

Conclusion

This chapter has discussed the role of data analysis in qualitative research studies. This means focusing on different ways data can be examined. The importance of analysing data was stated that highlighted the need to critically analyse data in a consistent way.

Review questions

1. Why is data analysis important in qualitative research?
2. What different ways can data be analysed?
3. What is the role of time in analysing data?

Suggested activity

Collect five articles on a topic you are interested in that have used a qualitative research approach. Then analyse how they have processed the data.

Web exercise

On the Internet type in the word 'qualitative data analysis' and see what comes up in the answer. Try and see if some of the results relate to specific topics or themes.

Multiple choice questions

1. What kind of research often asks the researcher to feel certain emotions?
   a. Quantitative
   b. Qualitative
   c. All of the above
   d. None of the above
2. What kind of research involves a tremendous amount of emotional energy?
   a. Conceptual
   b. Hypotheses tested
   c. Emotionally demanding
   d. None of the above
3. Interpretivism can be described as
   a. Understanding behaviour based on the context
   b. Statistically testing information
   c. Generating hypotheses
   d. None of the above
4. What kind of theory involves basing the analysis on existing theoretical frameworks?
   a. Empirical
   b. Qualitative
   c. Grounded
   d. Contextual
5. The process of coding data can be best described as
   a. Organising collected information
   b. Scrutinizing and pondering observations
   c. Relating observations to research questions
   d. All of the above

Answers
1. B, 2. C., 3. A, 4. C, 5. D

References

Gioia, D. A. (2004). A renaissance self: Prompting personal and professional revitalization. In *Renewing Research Practice: Scholars' Journeys*: 97–114, P. J. Frost & R. E. Stablein (Eds.). Stanford, CA: Stanford University Press.

Gioia, D. A. (2021). A systematic methodology for doing qualitative research. *The Journal of Applied Behavioral Science*, *57*(1), 20–29.

Gioia, D. A., & Chittipeddi, K. (1991). Sensemaking and sensegiving in strategic change initiation. *Strategic Management Journal*, *12*(6), 433–448.

Gioia, D. A., Corley, K. G., & Hamilton, A. L. (2013). Seeking qualitative rigor in inductive research: Notes on the Gioia methodology. *Organizational Research Methods*, *16*(1), 15–31.

Gioia, D. A., Price, K. P., Hamilton, A. L., & Thomas, J. B. (2010). Forging an identity: An insider–outsider study of processes involved in organizational identity formation. *Administrative Science Quarterly*, *55*(1), 1–46.

Guba, E. G., & Lincoln, Y. S. (1994). Competing paradigms in qualitative research. *Handbook of Qualitative Research*, *2*(163–194), 105.

Kiyimba, N. & O'Reilly, M. (2016). An exploration of the possibility for secondary traumatic stress among transcriptionists: A grounded theory approach, *Qualitative Research in Psychology*, *13*(1), 92–108.

Kumar, S., & Cavallaro, L. (2018). Researcher self-care in emotionally demanding research: A proposed conceptual framework. *Qualitative Health Research*, *28*(4), 648–658.

Langley, A. (1999). Strategies for theorizing from process data. *Academy of Management Review*, *24*(4), 691–710.

Lee, L. W., Dabirian, A., McCarthy, I. P., & Kietzmann, J. (2022). Making sense of text: Artificial intelligence-enabled content analysis. *European Journal of Marketing*, in Press.

Locke, K., Feldman, M., & Golden-Biddle, K. (2022). Coding practices and iterativity: Beyond templates for analyzing qualitative data. *Organizational Research Methods*, *25*(2), 262–284.

Pratt, M. G., Sonenshein, S., & Feldman, M. S. (2022). Moving beyond templates: A bricolage approach to conducting trustworthy qualitative research. *Organizational Research Methods*, *25*(2), 211–238.

Saldaña, J. (2016). Goodall's verbal exchange coding: An overview and example. *Qualitative Inquiry*, *22*(1), 36–39.

Westermann, A., & Forthmann, J. (2022). Social listening: A potential game changer in reputation management How big data analysis can contribute to understanding stakeholders' views on organisations. *Corporate Communications*, in press.

Further reading

Barney, J. B. (2018). Editor's comments: Positioning a theory paper for publication. *Academy of Management Review*, *43*, 345–348.

Barney, J. B. (2020). Contributing to theory: Opportunities and challenges. *AMS Review*, *10*, 49–55.

Batty, E. (2020). Sorry to say goodbye: The dilemmas of letting go in longitudinal research. *Qualitative Research*, *20*(6), 784–799.

Chrisman, J. J., Fang, H. C., & Steier, L. (2021). Positioning, articulating, and crafting conceptual articles on entrepreneurship. *Entrepreneurship Theory and Practice*, 10422587211057023. https://doi.org/10.1177/1042258721105702

Mason, W. (2021). On staying: Extended temporalities, relationships and practices in community engaged scholarship. *Qualitative Research*, 14687941211049318, in press.

Schwarz, G., & Stensaker, I. (2014). Time to take off the theoretical straightjacket and (re) introduce phenomenon-driven research. *Journal of Applied Behavioral Science*, *50*(4), 478–501.

Sheng, J., Amankwah-Amoah, J., Khan, Z., & Wang, X. (2021). COVID-19 pandemic in the new era of big data analytics: Methodological innovations and future research directions. *British Journal of Management*, *32*(4), 1164–1183.

Shepherd, D., & Williams, T. (2022). Does it need to be broader or deeper? Trade-offs in entrepreneurship theorizing, *Entrepreneurship Theory & Practice*, 1–28.

Sherry, E. (2013). The vulnerable researcher: Facing the challenges of sensitive research. *Qualitative Research Journal*, *13*, 278–288.

Strauss, A., & Corbin, J. (1998). *Basics of Qualitative Research*. New York: Sage.

Tracy, S. J. (2010). Qualitative quality: Eight "big tent" criteria for excellent qualitative research. *Quality Inquiry*, *16*(10), 837–851.

Van Burg, E., Cornelissen, J., Stam, W., & Jack, S. (2022). Advancing qualitative entrepreneurship research: Leveraging methodological plurality for achieving scholarly impact. *Entrepreneurship Theory and Practice*, *46*(1), 3–20.

Winfield, T. P. (2021). Vulnerable research: Competencies for trauma and justice-informed ethnography. *Journal of Contemporary Ethnography*, 08912416211017254, in press.

7

QUANTITATIVE BUSINESS MANAGEMENT RESEARCH METHODOLOGIES

Introduction

Quantitative research involves collecting data that includes numbers, facts and statistics. To collect this type of data normally surveys or questionnaires are utilised. This means the emphasis is on analysing patterns in order to determine behaviour.

Learning objectives

- To understand the reason for collecting quantitative data.
- To focus on the different types of quantitative data.
- To understand how to analyse quantitative data.

OPENING DISCUSSION QUESTION

Why do you think quantitative data analysis is important?

Surveys and questionnaire design

Mail surveys are often used due to respondents preferring a paper-based questionnaire. This means they obtain a physical copy of the questions but increasingly due to cost and efficiency reasons there have been more online surveys. The delay in mailing a survey then receiving the answers can be an issue in choosing whether to

DOI: 10.4324/9781003314516-7

conduct a mail survey. Often prepaid envelopes to return the survey are included when sending the questionnaire.

Online surveys offer a faster response time and enable answers to be exported quickly into excel files. This reduces data entry errors and enables an easier way to obtain responses. Designing an online survey takes time as there needs to be consideration for screen sizes. In addition, language issues meant that surveys will need to be translated into different languages.

Traditional survey methods such as using random phone numbers to ask questions no longer have the same effectiveness. Telephone surveys have decreased in importance as people communicate via web-based tools. In addition, due to privacy issues it is harder to gain access to respondents via telephone. This means researchers are searching for other ways to obtain good samples.

ARTICLE READING ANALYSIS

Read the following article about next-generation prediction metrics for composite-based PLS–SEM.

- Hair Jr, J. F., (2021), "Next-generation prediction metrics for composite-based PLS-SEM", Industrial Management & Data Systems, 121(1): 5–11.

Consider when reading the article about why prediction assessment tools are important in business management research. Write down how prediction metrics can be used to improve the overall findings of a study.

A questionnaire normally implies a set of written questions that a respondent is asked to answer. Sreejesh et al. (2014:143) define a questionnaire as "a set of questions to be asked from respondents in an interview, with appropriate instructions indicating which questions are to be asked, and in what order". It can be in a written or online format but increasingly is done online in order to make it easier to analyse the data. In the past written questionnaires were handed to people with the objective of obtaining their response to certain issues. Table 7.1 states the advantages and disadvantages of quantitative data methods.

Analytics

Business analytics is a way to encourage the development of data-driven research management techniques. Different types of analytics are referred to in different ways. For example, human resource analytics is commonly labelled as people analytics, human resource analytics, workforce analytics, talent analytics and human capital analysis (Margherita, 2022). Human resources analytics is defined as "the approach to managing people within organisations and making more objective,

TABLE 7.1 Advantages and disadvantages of quantitative data methods

Advantages	*Disadvantages*
1. Focuses on statistical inferences from collected data.	1. There is less personal interaction from data sources.
2. Enables extrapolations to be inferred from the data.	2. Means that the researcher needs to collect and then analyse through statistical packages the data.
3. Allows for an objective approach to data management.	3. Can be time intensive to collect the data.
4. Highlights how patterns can occur over time.	4. Can be expensive to analyse the data.
5. Stresses the need for large amounts of information to be obtained.	5. Large amounts of data are required.

rational and effective decisions about employees based on the analysis of data" (Margherita, 2022:1). This means it involves focusing on the way people behave based on statistical data. Thereby enabling more information to be obtained about human behaviour through the use of personal characteristics.

Analytics are used as a way to provide both diagnostic and predictive capabilities (Edwards & Edwards, 2019). Diagnostic capabilities refer to making decisions about why something has occurred. This can differ depending on the knowledge and expertise of the person making the diagnosis. Predictive capabilities refer to making estimates or guesses about what might occur in the future. This is hard to do as nobody knows what will definitely happen in the future. Approximations can be made in terms of suggestions but these guesses are subject to environmental change. In addition, there may be other factors that come into play that were not previously considered.

EXERCISE

Choose a type of organisation (e.g. fashion, sport) then design a study to collect data from multiple sources.

Experiments

Natural experiments involve taking an organic approach to what is emerging from the data. This means theories evolve in an ad-hoc way thereby allowing the researcher time to think about the findings. Interpretive methods refer to analysing the data based on the context in which it is occurring. This results in accepting that the data is useful when applied to a certain situation. Contextualised explanation means that the information obtained is based on the existing environment.

Thereby highlighting that the time and place in which the data was obtained is important.

Experiments can occur in a number of different settings but the main ones are laboratory, field and natural (Hsu et al., 2017). Laboratory settings occur in classrooms or other places that are deliberately set up for the experiment. This means they provide a controlled way to introduce different stimuli to participants. Thereby isolating the participants from other environmental factors. This means different stimuli can be used at different time points in order to evaluate behaviour. There has been a decrease in studies using laboratories due to online laboratories being established.

Field experiments occur in the real world. They typically examine the impact of different constraints on behaviour. They enable a more realistic context to study individual behaviour. They typically occur in a non-controlled environment such as a work place setting. This enables other factors such as gender rations to be examined.

Experiments are a popular methodology used in the psychology field. This is due to the way environments can be changed in order to test different interaction effects. In business management experiments have not been used much due to the popularity of other research methods. This is changing with more business studies integrating psychological topics.

The main way to conduct experiments is through conventional laboratory techniques. This means rooms are set up with the specific purpose to conduct an experiment. They enable multiple experiments to be conducted with different people and stimuli. The advantages of laboratory experiments is that they are not influenced as much by unintended stimuli compared to natural settings. The disadvantage is that the setting lacks a sense of reality that makes the findings hard to generalise.

EXERCISE

Why do you think people prefer quantitative data collection methods to qualitative data collection methods?

Bias in research studies

In any research study there should be some consideration of bias. Zhang and Cueto (2017:420) define bias as "the systematic deviation from rationale choice theory when people chose actions and estimate probabilities". Biases are prevalent in research due to researchers' cultural conditioning. This means research can display some acknowledged and unacknowledged biases. As many research articles in business management are written in English there is a bias towards English-speaking researchers. This has changed with more articles being published in other languages.

Zhang and Cueto (2017) suggest that bias in research is evident in the availability, escalation of commitment, overconfidence, overoptimism, illusion of control, the law of small numbers, representativeness, self-serving attribution, similarity, status quo and planning fallacy. Overconfidence means a person overestimates their research results. This means the actual results are not in line with comparable studies. This can limit the accuracy of their research. Overoptimism means that a researcher thinks that their research results show more than they do. This means stressing too much the positive results and neglecting weak effects. Self-serving attribution involves taking credit for successes whilst neglecting to mention failures. This is an issue when researchers want their results to show specific effects and may be under time pressures. As a consequence, they can deny responsibility for the results not showing what they want.

Illusion of control involves overemphasising what is done. This can include indicators that the researcher manipulated the research. This is evident in research that may now show direct relationships. The law of small numbers means that there is a small number of survey respondents and the results cannot be generalised. This means that the sample size is limited and not indicative of the overall population.

Similarity refers to research that has common characteristics to other reported research. This negates the authenticity of the research study. Availability refers to making sense of research findings based on what information is easy to access. This means making judgements that might not be true.

Representativeness refers to research that is presented in a way that makes it look like other research. This sense of familiarity results in others feeling comfortable about the findings. Status quo refers to using the same findings when the results may show something different. Planning fallacy refers to not acknowledging the time needed to do a task. This is common in research studies particularly amongst novice researchers. Escalation of commitment refers to researchers persisting despite having failures. This means they are not willing to change and pivot.

Zhang and Cueto (2017) suggest that there are three types of biases that depart from normative beliefs: make happy, sketchy attribute and psycho physics. The make-happy bias involves adopting a belief that the research results should be in a format to make others happy. This can involve not indicating negative evidence. Sketchy attribute bias involves focusing on one aspect of the research findings instead of acknowledging other findings. Psycho physics bias involves distorting the quantitative attributes of research. This means the perceived research findings are not in line with the actual results.

Social network analysis

Social network analysis focuses on the relationships between entities in society. This means it emphasises interactions instead of individual or group behaviour. It initially emerged from studies focused on anthropology and sociology due to the need to study behaviour over time. Originally the analysis was hard to do as it had to be depicted in diagrams or discussed in terms of relationships. Computational developments have made it easier to input the data into computer programs.

The key features of social network analysis is that it focuses on dynamic and evolving relationships. This differs to the focus on independent individuals acting due to self-interest in society. People act by themselves but are often influenced by social interactions. This means there is a relational perspective to individual behaviour. There are a number of interconnected individuals and entities in society that work together on business projects. This means focusing on social networks can be useful in understanding behaviour.

ARTICLE READING ANALYSIS

Read the article about expanding the scope for marketing research as a force for good in a sustainable world.

- Mende, M., & Scott, M. L. (2021). May the Force Be with You: Expanding the Scope for Marketing Research as a Force for Good in a Sustainable World. *Journal of Public Policy & Marketing, 40*(2), 116–125.

Think about why it is important to incorporate social and sustainability issues within methodological practices. As part of your reading consider how the 17 United Nations Sustainable Development goals can be incorporated into research practices.

Wäsche et al. (2017:139) describe a social network as "a catchphrase, not only in the context of social media, but also in academic writing as a metaphor for anything from alliances, coalitions, clusters and groups". This means social media as a word has gained popularity with the increased usage of social media in society. However, it has been in existence for a long time in academic circles. This is due to its usefulness in understanding relational linkages between entities that can help deliver value. Most consider social networks as a positive term for interactions that lead to value creation.

In social network analysis, the linkages between entities need to be made evident. This will help to understand how information is exchanged and why certain connections are maintained. The network under investigation needs to be delineated. This will make it easier to analyse due to certainty around the entities existing within it. In a network actors are usually called nodes as they are the entities that interact with others. The nodes are related to others through ties. These ties can be based on pre-existing relationships such as friendship or family associations or new interactions. Within a social network, the dyad is more than two nodes and their interactions. The dyad is the entity that is focused on during the social network analysis in order to assess how it is changing.

In social network analysis the nodes and ties are analysed. The ties can be direct or indirect depending on the type of relationship. Tie strength can be important in assessing how much information is shared. The main types of ties that are analysed in social network analysis are: similarities, social relations, interactions and flows (Hasche et al., 2017). Similarities involve common characteristics or associations between participants. This can include location, occupation or educational level. The similarities will differ for each social network depending on what is being analysed. Typically similarities provide a way of analysing common features that influence behaviour. They can include membership of the same association or belonging to a family. In addition, they can relate to a number of people having the same attitude or emotion. Social relations refer to how people interact with others in society. It can be based on knowing others due to work or family connections. Social relations can include cognitive relations in terms of being aware of certain people. This helps in understanding whether the social relations are conducted on a frequent or sporadic basis. Interactions are more loosely defined and refer to other people interacting within another person in a formal or informal manner. Flows refer to how quickly or slowly interactions occur. They can involve information being disseminated or be intermittent interactions.

ARTICLE READING ANALYSIS

Read the following article about offsite manufacturing research that discusses different types of methodologies.

- Ehwi, R. J., Oti-Sarpong, K., Shojaei, R., & Burgess, G. (2022). Offsite Manufacturing Research: A Systematic Review of Methodologies Used. *Construction Management and Economics, 40*(1), 1–24.

Think about how research methodologies are changing based on the topic of interest. Write down how new research data types and sources are being utilised in methodological practices.

Structural equation modelling

Structural equation modelling (SEM) is a popular statistical analysis technique used in business management studies. It is useful due to the way it enables the testing of relationships between variables. Holt et al. (2006:385) define SEM as a "multivariate statistical technique that tests relationships between observed and/or latent variables while incorporating potential measurement errors". The advantage of SEM over other statistical methods is that it can examine complex linkages amongst variables.

This enables more detailed information to be obtained about the direction and significance of relationships. This means that SEM can test for measurement error that is helpful in assessing the validity of relationships. Moreover, it enables a researcher to develop a conceptual model.

SEM allows for multiple independent and dependent relationships to be tested. The use of SEM in business management studies is popular due to the need to test theoretical models. SEM enables the testing of equivalence of measurement models across groups that is helpful in cross-country studies.

SEM can provide evidence of causality but does not prove causality. This means causal modelling is a feature of SEM and can help indicate reciprocal or one-directional relationships. In SEM the type of software used can result in different results. This is due to the computational variation and methods used in the software. Therefore, researchers normally report the type of software they used in the analysis and which version of the software was used.

There are two main subtypes of SEM: covariance and variance-based (Henseler, 2017). The difference between the two methods is based on how the data is analysed. Henseler (2017:179) states that "covariance-based SEM minimizes a discrepancy between the empirical covariance matrix implied by the structural equations of the specified model". This means it is important to analyse how the data is presented in the covariance matrix and how it relates to theory. In contrast the variance-based SEM focuses on construct scores as indicators of relationship strength. Henseler (2017:179) suggests that "variance-based SEM determines construct scores as linear combinations of observed variables such that a certain criterion of interrelatedness is maximized". Therefore, the emphasis is on the interrelationships amongst variables that are included in a study.

Chin et al. (2008:287) states SEM "simultaneously reflects a theoretical network of manifest (observed) variables and latent (unobserved) variables (constructs) as well as a general statistical technique". This means unlike multiple regression or other statistical techniques it allows for concurrent testing to be done. This means it is a versatile way to analyse data. To use SEM there needs to be a minimal sample size in order to allow for the relationships to be tested. Normally sample sizes of 100 or more are considered adequate but the minimal sample size required differs based on the discipline. For example, in the marketing discipline normally large sample sizes are preferred but in some management disciplines such as entrepreneurship the expected sample size can be smaller. SEM normally involves a five steps process: (1) model specification, (2) model identification, (3) model estimation, (4) model evaluation and (5) model respecification.

Cognitive mapping

Cognitive mapping is used as a way to understand cause–effect relationships amongst variables in a study. Simple cognitive maps are based on network relationships (Warren, 1995). Thereby enabling others to see how the variables in a study interact and the nature of the relationships. It is helpful to graphically depict how variables interact as a way of illustrating how the system works. Normally signs of influence such as + (positive) and – (negative) can be added to the map.

A cognitive map represents a mental representation of a subject matter. It is based on an individual's knowledge of a situation and their beliefs about the nature and extent of the interaction. Instead of relying on written words to communicate meanings, a cognitive map enables others to see relationships. Thereby enabling another way to communicate that interactions that are being derived from the data. Causality in terms of what variables influence other factors is important in a cognitive map. Causality can be described as whether a change in one variable influences another variable (Schneider et al., 1998). When a cognitive map is constructed, an individual will normally depict the nature of the interdependence between variables. Thereby enabling dynamics to be shown that are common in real-life situations.

Cognitive mapping can take place in a number of different ways. It can be conducted before data is collected and analysed in order to depict theorised relationships. It can be done whilst data is being collected as new information emerges. Or alternatively it can be done after data has been collected as a way of depicting relationships.

Cognitive maps can help support the interpretation of information through suggesting associations. Visually depicting data can be done through diagrams, maps or sketches. It is a useful way to communicate business information and can improve others understanding about data. Visualisation of data helps in synthesising information in an easier-to-understand manner. Thereby compressing information that might be difficult to describe in a written format.

Data that is graphically depicted can help people better understand the available information. Thereby reformulating their thought processes on what the data is saying. Data can be shown in various ways depending on a person's interpretation. This means it is subjective and based on a person's opinion. Due to individual differences, it can help if multiple people visually show their interpretation of the data. Each diagram can then be viewed and if needed compared to highlight the similarities and differences. When comparing diagrams each person can describe why and how they have depicted the data. This means exchanging information and knowledge. As a result, each person's diagram may change based on the feedback from others.

Visualisation of data has numerous benefits including helping build creativity. This can lead to novel and new perspectives about the relationships included in the analysed data. There are some risks associated with visualising data due to its subjective nature. This means there are computer programs to help researchers map their data. This can overcome challenges associated with visually representing data instead of verbally explaining it.

Cognitive mapping can help solve business problems by mapping knowledge. Normally nodes in a diagram are associated with concepts. There are then arrows or lines to link different concepts. This helps to map the cause and effect systems evident in the data. Cognitive mapping is a way to more understand relationships in more depth. It is a powerful way to depict data that leads to more discussion. Sometimes cognitive mapping is called mental models as it involves individuals depicting their thoughts.

Fuzzy set qualitative comparative analysis

Fuzzy set qualitative comparative analysis (FsQCA0 is defined as "an inductive, iterative method that reveals patterns in the data at the case level that tend to be obscured by symmetric methods" (Douglas & Prentice, 2019:70). The advantage of using FsQCA is that it does not require data symmetry or relationship symmetry. This means it is a more flexible way to understand relationships in the data. It enables interdependencies rather than just direct relationships to be examined.

FsQCA enables a more holistic way to examine data. The first step in fsQCA involves choosing what antecedent conditions need to be incorporated into the configural model. The conditions should be based on theoretical rationale that is substantiated by relevant literature. This can include empirical evidence that suggests a relationship between constructs. FsQCA is an iterative method, which means there needs to be a rationale for including certain conditions. This means it is inductive and relies on well-justified research.

The next step in the process involves calibrating the data. Ragin and Strand (2008) suggest that the calibrated score represents the true values that are associated with a statement. This means the data is calibrated based on relevant anchor points. This involves utilising existing knowledge and information about each variable.

FsQCA enables an analysis of the variance of phenomenon under investigation. This helps in exploring relationships between variables as well as observing other variables. This enables the identification of multiple pathways that lead to the same outcome as well as the interdependence of variables. Douglas et al. (2020:3) state that "fsQCA examines the relationships between and among the antecedent variables (referring to these variables as 'conditions'), and characterises cases as having a particular combination of conditions (referred to as a 'configuration') that associates with the focal outcomes". FsQCA can result in surprising findings that were previously unavailable in other analysis techniques. This is due to it being an abductive approach in terms of building on existing knowledge sources. It can be used in combination with other methodological approaches in terms of involving mixed methods.

Guidelines

1. Think about what you want to test from the research.
2. Do research on appropriate sample sizes.
3. Compare your research question to other published research questions.
4. Find out if there are publicly available databases.
5. Do a timeline for how you will collect and then analyse data.

Developing expertise

Try to read a new book chapter or article about quantitative data analysis on a frequent basis.

Pitch

Develop a 2–3 minute presentation about how quantitative research methodologies led to better insights into current phenomena.

Checklist

1. Figure out how many data collection sources are required.
2. Map out the data collection process.
3. Think about each step of the data collection and analysis process.
4. Write your methodology approach and include appropriate references prior to collecting the data.
5. Once data is collected try to quickly analyse data so that it can be published.

Conclusion

This chapter has examined the role of quantitative research methodologies in business management research. This meant focusing on the advantages of quantitative data analysis compared to other research methodologies. The ways data can be collected using quantitative approaches was stated and explained. Thereby contributing to a researchers understanding of statistical analysis in research studies.

Review questions

1. What different ways is there to analyse quantitative data?
2. Why would you use a quantitative methodology in business research?
3. What different steps or processes are needed in quantitative research methodologies?

Suggested activities

Design a quantitative study that results in more information being obtained about post COVID-19 conditions.

Web exercise

Go onto the Internet and type in 'quantitative business methods' and see what the results are. Then read one or two of the results.

Multiple choice questions

1. Questionnaires can be in what kind of format?
   a. Written
   b. Online
   c. Both a and b
   d. None of the above
2. Human resource analytics are also labelled as
   a. People analytics
   b. Workforce analytics
   c. Talent analytics
   d. All of the above
3. What type of analytics refers to the managing of people based on the analysis of data?
   a. Statistical
   b. Human resource
   c. Technology
   d. None of the above
4. What kind of capabilities refers to making estimates or guesses?
   a. Statistical
   b. Diagnostic
   c. Predictive
   d. None of the above
5. What kind of experiments involve taking an organic approach to what is emerging from the data?
   a. Natural
   b. Statistical
   c. Emergent
   d. None of the above

Answers
1. C, 2. D, 3. B., 4. C, 5. A

References

Chin, W., Peterson, R. A., & Brown, S.P. (2008). Structural equation modeling in marketing: Some practical reminders, *Journal of Marketing Theory and Practice*, *16*(4), 287–298.

Douglas, E. J., & Prentice, C. (2019). Innovation and profit motivations for social entrepreneurship: A fuzzy-set analysis. *Journal of Business Research*, *99*, 69–79.

Douglas, E. J., Shepherd, D. A., & Prentice, C. (2020). Using fuzzy-set qualitative comparative analysis for a finer-grained understanding of entrepreneurship. *Journal of Business Venturing*, *35*(1), 105970.

Edwards, M. R., & Edwards, K. (2019). *Predictive HR Analytics: Mastering the HR Metric.* London: Kogan Page Publishers.

Hasche, N., Linton, G., & O'berg, C. (2017). Trust in OI-the case of med-tech start-up. *European Journal of Innovation Management*, 20(1), 31–49.

Henseler, J. (2017). Bridging design and behavioral research with variance-based structural equation modeling, *Journal of Advertising, 46*(1), 178–192, DOI:10.1080/00913367.2017.1281780

Holt, G., Ketchen, D., Cui, A., Prud'homme, A., Seggie, S., Stanko, M., ... Cavusgil, S. (2006). An assessment of the use of structural equation modelling in international business research. *Research Methodology in Strategy and Management, 3*, 385–416.

Hsu, D. K., Simmons, S. A., & Wieland, A. M. (2017). Designing entrepreneurship experiments: A review, typology, and research agenda. *Organizational Research Methods, 20*(3), 379–412.

Margherita, A. (2022). Human resources analytics: A systematization of research topics and directions for future research. *Human Resource Management Review, 32*(2), 100795.

Ragin, C. C., & Strand, S. I. (2008). Using qualitative comparative analysis to study causal order: Comment on Caren and Panofsky (2005). Sociological Methods & *Research, 36*(4), 431–441.

Schneider, B., White, S. S., & Paul, M. C. (1998). Linking service climate and customer perceptions of service quality: Tests of a causal model. *Journal of applied Psychology, 83*(2), 150.

Sreejesh, S., Mohapatra, S., & Anusree, M. R. (2014). *Business Research Methods: An Applied Orientation*. Heidelberg: Springer.

Warren, K. (1995). Exploring competitive futures using cognitive mapping. *Long Range Planning, 28*(5), 10–21.

Wäsche, H., Dickson, G., Woll, A., & Brandes, U. (2017). Social network analysis in sport research: An emerging paradigm. *European Journal for Sport and Society, 14*(2), 138–165.

Zhang, S. X., & Cueto, J. (2017). The study of bias in entrepreneurship. *Entrepreneurship Theory and Practice, 41*(3), 419–454.

Further reading

Barney, J. (2018). Editor's comments: Theory contributions and the AMR review process. *Academy of Management Review, 43*, 1–4. https://doi.org/10.5465/amr.2017.0540

Koronios, K., Dimitropoulos, P., Travlos, A., Douvis, I., & Ratten, V. (2020). Online technologies and sports: A new era for sponsorship. *The Journal of High Technology Management Research, 31*(1), 100373.

Martin, C. J. H., & Fleming, V. (2010). A 15-step model for writing a research proposal. *British Journal of Midwifery, 18*(12), 791–798.

Miragaia, D. A., Ferreira, J., & Ratten, V. (2017). Corporate social responsibility and social entrepreneurship: Drivers of sports sponsorship policy. *International Journal of Sport Policy and Politics, 9*(4), 613–623.

Mukherjee, D., Lim, W., Kumar, S., & Donthu, N. (2022). Guidelines for advancing theory and practice through bibliometric research. *Journal of Business Research, 148*, 101–115.

Ratten, V. (2020). Sport technology: A commentary. *The Journal of High Technology Management Research, 31*(1), 100383.

Ratten, V., Dana, L. P., & Ramadani, V. (2017). Internationalisation of family business groups in transition economies. *International Journal of Entrepreneurship and Small Business, 30*(4), 509–525.

Ratten, V., & Tajeddini, K. (2019). Entrepreneurship and sport business research: Synthesis and lessons: Introduction to the special journal issue. *International Journal of Sport Management and Marketing, 19*(1/2), 1–7.

8

BIBLIOMETRICS AND LITERATURE REVIEWS IN BUSINESS MANAGEMENT

Introduction

This chapter discusses the role of bibliometrics and literature reviews in business management studies. In recent times there has been a growth in interest in these types of methodologies as they enable a way to analyse the development of a topic in the literature (Aguinis et al., 2011). This means uncovering the most relevant authors and journals in a specific field of knowledge (Borenstein & Higgins, 2013). This chapter discusses how systematic reviews and bibliometrics are conducted and the steps required. This includes reviewing the literature in a way that summarises the main findings.

Learning objectives

- To understand how to do a bibliometric analysis.
- To review different types of bibliometric techniques.
- To highlight how literature can be reviewed in a systematic way.

> **OPENING DISCUSSION QUESTION**
>
> Why do you think there has been a growth in bibliometric and literature review studies?

DOI: 10.4324/9781003314516-8

Systematic literature reviews

Literature reviews can manifest in many different forms depending on the interests of the researcher (Grewal et al., 2018). Typically they are published as stand-alone articles but they are often used within other studies. Systematic literature reviews are a way to comprehensively analyse the main findings about a certain topic (Geyskens et al., 2009). They enable the reader to learn about the accumulated findings in a short period of time. Thereby making it easier and more time efficient than reading each article (Duval & Tweedie, 2000). Kraus et al. (2020:1024) define a traditional literature review as "non-structured, -systematic, or -transparent reviews with a higher level of subjectivity in data-collection and data-interpretation". Literature reviews are an important component of any article as they provide an overview of the current research on the topic (Higgins et al., 2009). They provide a way for researchers to demonstrate their knowledge of a topic and to indicate research gaps (Rowley & Paul, 2021).

The purpose of a systematic literature review is to systematically analyse each research output in the same way, which enables the data to be compared in terms of similar and different findings (Paul et al., 2021). A general literature review just discusses what the research is saying but a systematic one does it in a methodological way. Lim et al. (2022) suggest that literature reviews can play a supportive and facilitative role in research. The supportive role means that the literature review helps explain why a topic is important based on previous research studies. This means the literature review is used as a way of understanding the reason for the research and how the current study relates to other published studies (Siddaway et al., 2019). The facilitative role means that it enables others to read why a particular study is useful. This means it identifies the main streams of research in terms of research methodology and findings (Steel et al., 2021). This enables a comparison to be made about emerging areas of inquiry.

The benefit of conducting a systematic literature review is that it provides a scientific way to analyse research. This means collecting information but also reviewing it for meaning. They are useful for researchers to identify the main gaps and to predict trends. Thereby allowing the reader to obtain an analysis of the current state of the literature.

EXERCISE

Choose a topic you are interested in then conduct a 10-year review on research related to that topic.

Systematic literature reviews are subjective in nature as the researcher chooses which articles to review. This means they are subject to the interpretation of the person conducting the review. Literature reviews are conducted with the goal of logically including relevant studies. This means grouping research based on commonalities such as theme, methodology or results. Systematic literature reviews integrate the extant literature to make it easier for people to understand what has already been done and how they can contribute to the field.

Systematic literature reviews are recognised for the way they develop a holistic understanding about a topic. They do this by being a form of review-based research as the author(s) review previously published material. Paul and Criado (2020) suggest that systematic literature reviews can be classified as (1) domain-based: structured, framework-based, bibliometric, hybrid, review aiming for theory development, (2) theory-based review, (3) method-based and (4) meta analytical.

In domain-based reviews the focus is on the topic so there are different ways of conducting the analysis. A structured review follows the same steps and procedures to analyse each research item. This means having charts and tables that enable easy comparison between research items. The idea behind a structured review is that readers get the information in a certain way that makes it easier to understand. This enables each part of a research item in terms of structure to be compared. For example, the theories and methodologies utilised are stated in the same format. This type of format is normally the most popular due to the way it presents information.

A framework-based review utilises a set structure in order to present the results. This can include Paul and Benito's (2018) suggestion of using the antecedents, decision and outcomes. Therefore, the review is set out based on a previously developed framework. By doing so, they enable the research to be analysed in a certain way. Callahan (2014) suggested that the 6W framework (who, when, where, how, what and why) could be utilised to analyse research. By setting out the framework early on in a literature review it can provide a better understanding of the topic under investigation. New frameworks to analyse literature are constantly being developed. This makes it a useful way of deciphering the overall meaning of each research study (Table 8.1).

TABLE 8.1 Advantages and disadvantages of bibliometrics and literature reviews

Advantages	*Disadvantages*
1. Enables patterns to be analysed over time.	1. Can be difficult to learn the process of how to do a literature review.
2. Allows for the most popular articles and books to be acknowledged.	2. Requires knowledge of bibliometric software.
3. Shows how keywords and other article data changes over time.	3. Researchers need to focus on a key topic or journal to do the analysis.
4. Highlights under researched areas in need of further exploration.	4. The data once analysed needs to be interpreted.
5. Enables trends to be used for future research analysis.	5. Requires the data to be put into readable charts and tables.

How to conduct a literature review

A bibliometric review utilises statistical methods to find out information. This method is popular as it provides a way to understand the main citation and co-citations of published research. Therefore, the trends around the research can be tracked in order to project future output. There are different statistical packages used to conduct bibliometric reviews including Visualisation of Similarities (VoS).

Research schools are increasingly teaching students how to use these software packages in the early stages of their courses. This enables them to carry out bibliometric reviews and to incorporate the findings into their own research. There is a tendency to focus only on scientific articles in bibliometric analysis thereby neglecting books and book chapters. Moreover, the data obtained from a bibliometric analysis can quickly become outdated as new research is published. For this reason, most authors of bibliometric research state the date when the review was conducted. In addition, there is a tendency to focus on numbers and graphs rather than the findings. This means the review emphasises numerical counts rather than elaborating on research findings.

Academic research is built on advancing the ideas of others and implementing new ideas. Therefore, to increase the body of knowledge on a topic, a systematic literature review is needed. This will enable new research propositions and hypotheses to be advanced. In order to compare different points of time, a systematic literature review should use the same repeatable steps. This will make it a reliable source of information.

In order to conduct a literature review there needs to be an initial inclusion criterion for the studies that are sought. This normally means typing certain words or phrases into search engines in order to obtain results. Normally the search term will be the core concept of the field under investigation. For example, for studies on sport entrepreneurship the words sport and entrepreneurship, sport and innovation or sport and change might be typed into the search box. Alternatively, a manual review of studies can be conducted by reading the table of contents of journal articles to identify relevant articles. When searching for articles on a topic, there needs to be careful consideration of what words and terms to search for. This is due to there being some subjectivity around the inclusion of certain concepts. For example, some people think entrepreneurship and innovation are the same when in reality they are different topics. This means when writing up the results of a literature review, the author(s) should state which words they searched for. This will help the reader to better understand how the search was conducted.

In the inclusion criteria normally only journals are reviewed but due to increasing number of books and book chapters being Scopus indexed, they now are often counted in the search. There is a tendency to focus just on English language source as most journals are published in English. However, this too is changing with more non-English language journals becoming available. Moreover, online translation tools make it easier to translate articles into English. In the past, many relevant studies of certain topics were overlooked or not found. This limited the overall reliability of the literature review and mean there was a bias towards English language journals.

When conducting a search for articles people tend to use Googlescholar as it is an easy-to-use search engine. There are also other ways to find relevant articles and this includes using databases such as Proquest and Web of Science. Once the articles have been obtained they are normally downloaded and stored in fields or printed as hard copies. Each article is then read for relevance in order to ensure it is relevant. Normally researchers will write down details about the article including the author, article title, year of publication, type of article (e.g. conceptual, empirical) and main findings. Some researchers might further categorise the article by colour coding it or making note of its other features.

When searching for articles normally all articles relevant are sought but some people might refine it based on specific time periods. For example, the past ten, twenty or fifty years. Each article needs to be analysed in order to make sure there are no duplicates. The abstracts of each article are normally read first in order to analyse the content of the article. When conducting a literature review there can be just one person reading the abstract or a team of researchers. Depending on the number of articles found, it might be useful to have a number of people reading each article.

After the articles have been found then a quality assessment on each article might be done. Some literature reviews only focus on A level of highly ranked journals whilst other reviews include all relevant articles. Thus, there is a range of approaches that researchers can take in order to ascertain the quality of an article. Some use Scopus or Web of Science indexed journals as a quality metric.

In order to make the review process more transparent and trustworthy it can be useful for two reviewers to work in tandem then to compare their findings. This will enable any discrepancies or differences in opinion to be discussed. Moreover, it will enable a more detailed analysis of each article. Some articles might then be excluded based on their content or lack of content. This often applies when the article might really be a technical report or book review rather than a peer-reviewed journal article.

The review process of suitable articles will take some time as iterations are made. After finalising the articles to be included in the review, certain types of information will be taken from each article. This information normally involves detail about the content and findings of the study. Some people do this in a handwritten format whilst others type the information into a word document or computer program.

Document analysis is helpful in understanding the context of a research study. Bowen (2009:27) defines document analysis as "a systematic procedure for reviewing or evaluating documents-both printed and electronic (computer-based and Internet-transmitted) material". Documents can yield additional information that cannot be obtained in other ways. Moreover, documents enable people to learn more about a topic of interest. Often the knowledge is obtained in a serendipitous way and is unplanned. Documents are facts that can be shared with others. They enable others to consult written information to understand what has occurred in society. There are many different kinds of documents. Bowen (2009:27) states that documents can include

> advertisements; agendas, attendance registers, and minutes of meetings; manuals, background papers; books and brochures; diaries and journals; event programs (i.e. printed outlines); letters and memoranda; maps and charts; newspapers (clippings/articles); press releases; program proposals, application forms, and summaries; radio and television program scripts; organisational or institutional reports; survey data; and various public records.

EXERCISE

What is the difference between systematic literature reviews and bibliometric reviews?

Critical literature reviews

Critical literature reviews are a distinct category of literature reviews as they focus on analysing research studies. Not all literature reviews are critical as many just provide a summary of the current state of the literature on a topic. It is important to critically engage with the existing literature as a way of highlighting its positive and negative points.

A critique involves questioning what has been done with the view of improving its quality. This is useful in suggesting alternative perspectives about research findings. Being critical means asking questions about why and how things are done. This enables new information and viewpoints to come to light that can make a difference to how the research is perceived. Thereby by providing a critical analysis it can lead to new theories emerging in the literature. Wright and Michailova (2022:2) state that "the Greek term 'kritikos' means to judge, to discern, to make sense, to recognise, and to comprehend". These words are useful for understanding how critical analysis is done and why it is needed by researchers. To judge involves assessing whether something is right or wrong. People make assessments all the time based on their views. Some people will judge research differently based on their experience and knowledge of the topic. This means researchers need to keep an open mind when critically analysing research by focusing on the advantages and disadvantages of research methodologies. Research can be done in a number of different ways, so judgements about how it is done need to consider time and resource constraints.

To discern means to understand how the research was completed. This can involve comparing it to previous research studies and then evaluating it based on specific criteria. This will enable the reader to make sense of what occurred and to evaluate its quality. By doing so readers will recognise good from bad quality research by how the methodology is explained. This will enable others to comprehend the value of the research.

Meta analysis

Meta analysis provides a way to analyse a large number of articles on a certain theme. Paul and Barari (2022:1) define a meta analysis as "a research method for systematically combining and synthesising findings from multiple quantitative studies in a research domain". This means a meta analysis is based on the results of quantitative studies. Thereby focusing on the statistical results and findings. Compared to a literature review a meta analysis focuses on statistically analysing differences between studies. By doing so they emphasis certain characteristics of each article, book or book chapter that can provide a more holistic understanding of a research field.

Meta analyses use to be the preferred way to analyse a collection of research studies or topic areas. However, in recent years systematic literature reviews have become more popular. The reason for this is due to a need to discuss in written format a specific topic. This enables more information to be obtained on classifications and major themes evident in a research study.

ARTICLE READING ANALYSIS

1. Read the article about how neuromarketing can add value to traditional marketing research.

    - Meyerding, S. G., & Mehlhose, C. M. (2020). Can neuromarketing add value to the traditional marketing research? An exemplary experiment with functional near-infrared spectroscopy (fNIRS). *Journal of Business Research, 107*, 172–185.

Consider whether new technology offers a way to obtain hidden information that was previously difficult to obtain. Think about how neuromarketing can add value to existing research practices.

Bibliometrics

Bibliometric studies in order to be useful need to extend the discussion of the topic beyond the statistics. This means quantitative measures and analysis needs to be supported by detailed discussion. Thereby requiring the continued acceptance of such studies is dependent on how it contributes to the literature and practice. Bibliometric studies have been criticised for their focus on numbers rather than the narrative. This is not surprising given the emphasis in bibliometric studies on reporting statistical findings.

Bibliometric data can provide powerful analytical insights that can help guide future research. This is needed in order to understand where the field is and what needs to be done. Without conducting any form of bibliometric analysis there is no way to know how it has evolved. Bibliometrics provide reliable data that shows the current stage of knowledge.

Bibliometric analysis involves science mapping of the current literature in terms of citation analysis. It is a form of systematic literature review but focuses more on statistics. The idea behind a bibliometric analysis is that it is an objective way to analyse the literature. This differs to literature reviews that rely on subjective interpretations of the data. Thus, due to the need to manually code and analyse articles in a literature review, bibliometrics relies on technology. Thereby utilising technology in an efficient and time-friendly manner. This enables more information to be analysed and reviewed.

Mukherjee et al. (2022) suggest that bibliometric research can be conducted based on a domain, method or theory. A domain can include a context, construct, discipline, field or outlet (Mukherjee et al., 2022). A construct such as marketing orientation or entrepreneurial intensity is often used as a way to measure a topic. However, continued usage of the construct without analysing the findings might be detrimental. This means it is useful to step back and analyse the literature through a bibliometric study to find out what is happening. This can lead to further refinements and alterations if needed.

A context refers to a certain geographic location (e.g. Australia) or situation (e.g. COVID-19 pandemic). This enables studies related to the context to be analysed in detail. Often a topic might be analysed instead of the context so it is important to focus on both. This requires a better understanding about how environmental trends influence the literature. A discipline such as entrepreneurship can be analysed in detail in order to understand its development. This will help in understanding how it has developed and what might happen in the future. Thereby taking stock of what has been done in order to derive more fruitful future analysis. A field refers to a specific body of work around a certain topic. For example, sport entrepreneurship is a field of research that combines entrepreneurship and sport management studies. It is a field as there is a substantial amount of material existing on the topic. An outlet refers to where the research has been published such as a book, book chapter or journal article.

Pitch

Develop a 2–3 minute presentation that summarises the main steps needed to do a bibliometric review.

Guidelines

1. Know what specific topic you want to research before conducting the review.
2. Try to focus on a niche subject that can be easily distinguished from other subjects.
3. Read previous reviews before conducting your review.
4. Try to follow the structure or process used by other researchers.
5. Write up your analysis soon after it has been completed.

Developing expertise

In order to learn more about bibliometrics and literature reviews try to read previously published articles on the topic.

Checklist

1. Find out whether other bibliometrics have been done on your topic.
2. Review existing articles on your topic that are in a systematic review format.
3. Try to read methodology articles about systematic literature reviews.
4. Think about the time frame for your review.
5. Consider new research that relates to your topic.

Conclusion

This chapter has examined the role of bibliometrics and systematic literature reviews in business management research. Increasingly these kinds of research techniques are used in order to provide an overview of a field. This enables researchers to understand what has been conducted in the field and to suggest future research suggestions.

Review questions

1. What is a bibliometric analysis?
2. How does a bibliometric analysis differ to a systematic literature review?
3. What different types of literature reviews can be conducted?

Suggested activity

Read 2–3 bibliometric articles and consider their strengths and weaknesses.

Web exercise

Choose a topic then research online whether any previous bibliometric or literature reviews have been conducted on the same topic

Multiple choice questions

1. A traditional literature review is best defined as
   a. A systematic or transparent review
   b. Has a higher level of subjectivity in data collection
   c. Is non-structured
   d. All of the above
2. What are the main types of systematic literature reviews?
   a. Domain based
   b. Theory based
   c. Method based and meta analysis
   d. All of the above
3. Domain-based reviews include
   a. Meta analytical
   b. Structured, framework based, bibliometric, hybrid, review aiming for theory development
   c. Method based
   d. Theory based
4. The 6W framework to analyse research refers to
   a. Who, when, where, how, what, why
   b. Which method, why, how come
   c. Six whys
   d. None of the above
5. A statistical package used to conduct bibliometric reviews is:
   a. VOS (visualisation of similarity)
   b. SEM
   c. AMOS
   d. None of the above

Answers
1. D, 2. D, 3. B, 4. A, 5. A

References

Aguinis, H., Pierce, C. A., Bosco, F. A., Dalton, D. R., & Dalton, C. M. (2011). Debunking myths and urban legends about meta-analysis. *Organizational Research Methods*, *14*(2), 306–331.

Borenstein, M., & Higgins, J. P. T. (2013). Meta-analysis and subgroups. *Prevention Science*, *14*(2), 134–143.

Bowen, G. (2009). Document analysis as a qualitative research method. *Qualitative Research Journal*, *9*(2), 27–40.

Callahan, J. L. (2014). Writing literature reviews: A reprise and update. https://doi.org/10.1177/1534484314536705

Duval, S., & Tweedie, R. (2000). Trim and fill: A simple funnel-plot-based method of testing and adjusting for publication bias in meta-analysis. *Biometrics*, *56*(2), 455–463.

Geyskens, I., Krishnan, R., Steenkamp, J.-B. E., & Cunha, P.V. (2009). A review and evaluation of meta-analysis practices in management research. *Journal of Management, 35*(2), 393–419.

Grewal, D., Puccinelli, N., & Monroe, K. B. (2018). Meta-analysis: Integrating accumulated knowledge. *Journal of the Academy of Marketing Science, 46*(1), 9–30.

Higgins, J. P., Thompson, S. G., & Spiegelhalter, D. J. (2009). A reevaluation of random-effects meta-analysis. *Journal of the Royal Statistical Society: Series A (Statistics in Society), 172*(1), 137–159.

Kraus, S., Breier, M., & Dasí-Rodríguez, S. (2020). The art of crafting a systematic literature review in entrepreneurship research. *International Entrepreneurship and Management Journal, 16*(3), 1023–1042.

Lim, W. M., Kumar, S., & Ali, F. (2022). Advancing knowledge through literature reviews: 'what', 'why', and 'how to contribute'. *The Service Industries Journal, 42*(7–8), 481–513.

Mukherjee, D., Lim, W. M., Kumar, S., & Donthu, N. (2022). Guidelines for advancing theory and practice through bibliometric research. *Journal of Business Research, 148*, 101–115.

Paul, J., & Barari, M. (2022). Meta-analysis and traditional systematic literature reviews—What, why, when, where, and how? *Psychology & Marketing*, in press.

Paul, J., & Benito, G. R. (2018). A review of research on outward foreign direct investment from emerging countries, including China: What do we know, how do we know and where should we be heading? *Asia Pacific Business Review, 24*(1), 90–115.

Paul, J., & Criado, A. R. (2020). The art of writing literature review: What do we know and what do we need to know? *International Business Review, 29*(4), 101717.

Paul, J., Lim, W. M., O'Cass, A., Hao, A. W., & Bresciani, S. (2021). Scientific procedures and rationales for systematic literature reviews (SPAR-4-SLR). *International Journal of Consumer Studies, 45*(4), O1–O16.

Rowley, C., & Paul, J. (2021). Introduction: The role and relevance of literature reviews and research in the Asia Pacific. *Asia Pacific Business Review, 27*, 1–5.

Siddaway, A. P., Wood, A. M., & Hedges, L.V. (2019). How to do a systematic review: A best practice guide for conducting and reporting narrative reviews, meta-analyses, and meta-syntheses. *Annual Review of Psychology, 70*, 747–770.

Steel, P. D., Beugelsdijk, S., & Aguinis, H. (2021). The anatomy of an award-winning meta-analysis: Recommendations for authors, reviewers, and readers of meta-analytic reviews. *Journal of International Business Studies, 52*(1), 23–44.

Wright, A., & Michailova, S. (2022). Critical literature reviews: A critique and actionable advice. *Management Learning*, 13505076211073961.

Further reading

Barari, M., Ross, M., Thaichon, S., & Surachartkumtonkun, J. (2021). A meta-analysis of customer engagement behaviour. *International Journal of Consumer Studies, 45*, 457–477.

Borenstein, M., Hedges, L.V., Higgins, J. P., & Rothstein, H. R. (2021). *Introduction to Meta-Analysis*. New York: Wiley.

Littell, J. H., Corcoran, J., & Pillai, V. (2008). *Systematic Reviews and Metaanalysis*. Oxford: Oxford University Press.

Marshall, I. J., & Wallace, B. C. (2019). Toward systematic review automation: A practical guide to using machine learning tools in research synthesis. *Systematic Reviews, 8*(1), 1–10.

Moher, D., Liberati, A., Tetzlaff, J., Altman, D. G., & Group, P. (2009). Preferred reporting items for systematic reviews and meta-analyses: The PRISMA statement. *PLoS Medicine, 6*(7), e1000097.

Steel, P. D., & Kammeyer-Mueller, J. D. (2002). Comparing meta-analytic moderator estimation techniques under realistic conditions. *Journal of Applied Psychology*, *87*(1), 96–111.

Steel, P. D., Kammeyer-Mueller, J. D., & Paterson, T. A. (2015). Improving the meta-analytic assessment of effect size variance with an informed Bayesian prior. *Journal of Management*, *41*(2), 718–743.

Xiao, Y., & Watson, M. (2019). Guidance on conducting a systematic literature review. *Journal of Planning Education and Research*, *39*(1), 93–112.

9

UNITED NATIONS SUSTAINABLE DEVELOPMENT GOALS AND RESEARCH ENGAGEMENT

Introduction

This chapter discusses how the United Nations Sustainable Development goals influence research practices. Each goal will be reviewed in terms of its relevance for business management practices. This will help researchers consider which goal might be best suited for their research needs.

Learning objectives

- To understand why sustainable development goals are relevant to research.
- To link the sustainable development goals to business research.
- To analyse the current and future sustainable development goals with regards to business management.

Sustainable development goals

The sustainable development goals have been established in order to preserve current environmental conditions for future generations (Avelar et al., 2019). This means each goal is interrelated but relates to a distinct objective (Bali Swain & Yang-Wallentin, 2020). This includes issues around business, the environment and society. By integrating each goal with other goals it helps to create global partnerships (Di Vaio et al., 2020). Researchers are being asked to map how their research fits into these sustainable development goals (Dana & Ratten, 2017). On many universities web pages it states which goal a researcher is aligned with and in some cases maps each research publication to a specific goal.

DOI: 10.4324/9781003314516-9

DISCUSSION QUESTION

Why do you think the sustainable development goals are important to business management researchers?

Integrating the sustainable development goals into research enables more practical conclusions to be made about the relevance of the research. This enables policymakers and practitioners to understand the rationale and motivation for the research. The sustainable development goals have deliberately been developed in order to provide broad and holistic ways about how sustainability can be incorporated into business activities. This is important for business management researchers who need to show the relationship between their research and how it provides a benefit to the business community. Table 9.1 states the advantages and disadvantages of the sustainable development goals to business management research.

No poverty

The first goal relates to ending poverty in all its forms everywhere in the world. This goal is hard to achieve due to the varying levels of economic development of countries (Hickel, 2019). Some countries have a high standard of living due to their status as developed countries whilst other countries are classified as developing as they are still yet to meet economic objectives (Giannetti et al., 2020).

TABLE 9.1 Advantages and disadvantages of sustainable development goals

Advantages	*Disadvantages*
1. Enables researchers to consider the sustainability implications of their research.	1. Can be difficult to align research to a sustainable development goal.
2. Allows for different research to be counted towards a specific development goal.	2. The sustainable development goals may change in the future necessitating business researchers to rethink their research practices.
3. Connects business management research to sustainable development.	3. It can result in too much focus on sustainable issues.
4. Highlights specific sustainable development goals discussed in research.	4. Can be hard to link the research to one specific sustainable development goal.
5. Enables researchers to think about the connections of their research to society.	5. The goals might be updated in the future.

During the COVID-19 pandemic there was a rise in poverty levels. Post the COVID-19 pandemic these poverty levels are expected to again rise due to growth in inflation. Poverty can be defined in different ways but normally refers to quality of life in terms of how much a person requires to live a good life. It can also relate to access to essential services such as good food, heating and cooling as well as educational services. The way poverty is defined has changed due to perceptions about its meaning altering in society (Mio et al., 2020).

Zero hunger

The second goal relates to zero hunger. This relates to a need to feed people regardless of their income level and accessibility to food products. There has recently been an increase in inflation rates that has led to a rise in food prices. This has meant some necessary food items such as fruit and vegetables has increased. In addition, there has been a shift towards healthy eating. This has meant a rising interest in nutrition and how food influences a person's health. As a consequence, in many countries there is an emphasis on dairy products such as yoghurt and cheese due to their vitamin components. This has led to many innovative food products being developed to cater for these markets (Ratten & Ferreira, 2017). Related to this development is the growth in interest in infant formula and other milk powder formulas for certain age groups. Recently in the United States there was a shortage of baby formula that resulted in an increased interest in food security. Milk powder formula is often used as a way to meet nutritional requirements that are not being met through the ingestion of other foods. This helps people obtain vitamins and other nutrients that have health benefits.

Food security is a major issue for many countries particularly those with a high number of people living in urban areas. This has led to an emphasis on importing food rather than producing their own food. As a consequence, when there are global crises such as the COVID-19 pandemic this can lead to delays in supply chains.

There have been innovations in how and where food can be grown. This has led to an increased emphasis in sustainable agricultural methods (Rashid & Ratten, 2020). In the past, food was grown via traditional methods using soil and land but now there are new ways to grow food. This is changing the way people consume food. More people are buying vitamins and this is linked to an increased general interest in nutrition. The range of vitamins has changed with new types of products continually entering the market. This includes products such as ginseng and green tea that were previously used in Chinese medicine but have since gained mainstream market acceptance. In addition, more attention has been placed on food waste. This is due to the realisation that unused food could be used for other purposes. This can include giving unused food to people in need or using it as an input in other products such as powering a car or other electronic equipment.

ARTICLE READING ANALYSIS

Read the following article about sustainable development and the strategic role of business.

- Mio, C., Panfilo, S., & Blundo, B. (2020). Sustainable development goals and the strategic role of business: A systematic literature review. *Business Strategy and the Environment, 29*(8), 3220–3245.

After reading the article consider how the sustainable development goals are changing based on societal trends. As part of your consideration think about why businesses are more interested in achieving the sustainable development goals.

Good health and wellbeing

The third goal focuses on good health and wellbeing, which is related to goals one and two. Good health is linked to increased societal awareness about the role people's lifestyle plays in their overall wellbeing (Moyer & Hedden, 2020). People are living longer so they are placing more attention on their health. This also relates to an increase in some people's leisure time. Healthy living can refer to where a person lives in terms of their access to parkland and other greenery or in terms of their general psychological wellbeing. There is more emphasis on a person's mental health in terms of their emotional stability. This has resulted in more people becoming interested in mediation and other relaxing techniques. Due to medical advances, there has been many associated health changes such as IVF treatment that have revolutionised the healthcare industry. One of the major health issues concerning global health systems at the moment is the long-term effect of COVID-19. In addition, there is a concern about the impact of the COVID-19 pandemic on other sectors of the economy particularly around hospitality and tourism.

Quality education

The fourth goal relates to quality education. This means emphasising knowledge acquisition through different kinds of learning activities. Quality education has changed in meaning due to different kinds of knowledge development being emphasised. In some countries financial literacy is important whilst in others creativity is thought to be a critical skill. In addition, different kinds of skills such as ingenuity and critical problem solving are being taught.

More people are now going to higher education institutions such as university and TAFE. This has lengthened the time students spend studying but has enabled more in-depth knowledge to be acquired. As a consequence, more students now have postgraduate degrees and this is enhancing their employability. This change in educational preferences means new educational practices such as remote learning need to be introduced.

People are now expected to be lifelong learners. This means they are continually learning new things. As a result, micro-credentialing and other short courses have become popular. This enables people to obtain knowledge about specific things. New technological innovations particularly around digital learning have become popular.

Gender equality

The fifth goal relates to gender equality particularly in terms of female empowerment. This goal can be controversial due to entrenched behaviour. This means it is important to try and achieve gender equality by promoting better policies. This can include the participation rates of different genders in certain occupations and industry fields.

In the past certain professions such as hairdressers tended to be associated with specific genders. This limited the ability of females and males to enter these professions. This has changed with the introduction of educational policies designed to bring about equality. This is particularly evident in the engineering and science fields where there has been a deliberate effort to increase female participation rates.

The COVID-19 pandemic resulted in a change in gender parity due to students studying from home and people working remotely. This limited the ability of women but also men to pursue different career objectives. It can be hard to achieve gender equality due to cultural, social and religious practices. This means it is important that discrimination based on gender does not occur. Governments need to implement safeguards to protect people based on their gender. This can include monitoring equality and other related enforcement requirements. As part of this goal there has been an emphasis on eliminating violence against women. This can include changing societal views about appropriate behaviour.

As part of the gender equality target, there has been increased recognition about the value of unpaid work. This can include people who volunteer for non-profit organisations. This can ensure more knowledge is obtained about the role different genders play in public life and social decision making.

Clean water and sanitation

The sixth goal relates to clean water and sanitation. Increasing emphasis is being placed on people having access to clean water (Schroeder et al., 2019). This is due to the pollution and contamination of some groundwater having health effects. Clean drinking water is needed due to its association with quality of life. In addition, there is more emphasis around clean water in rivers and oceans. This means less pollution flowing into rivers from factories and more emphasis on sustainability (Van der

Waal & Thijssens, 2020). There has recently been a change in the use of single-use plastics to paper-based formats. This is due to throwaway cups and bags going into the ocean and influencing the marine habitat.

Some countries have enough drinking water for their population whilst other countries are dependent on water from outside sources. This influences how much money people pay for water services. There are desalination plants that convert saltwater to freshwater in many locations. Moreover, households have water containers that enable them to collect rainwater that is then used for other purposes. Due to deforestation and mining the land and water tables have changed. This has led to a lack of suitable drinking water and water for farm usage. Innovations are changing this with the replantation of forests and ability to reinvigorate land.

Affordable and clean energy

This goal relates to the ability of people to have access to reliable and sustainable energy. Affordability has become a key political issue around the world due to rising energy prices. The Ukrainian/Russian conflict has led to a surge in energy prices that have led to price increases for other products and services. As many energy companies were deregulated the prices are market based. This means in many cases they are not subsidised by the government although this is changing with rebates being introduced. Sustainable energy is becoming a global priority due to global warming and the need to rely on alternative energy sources. This has resulted in a change from petrol to electrical cars. Moreover, solar and wind power are becoming more popular.

Decent work and economic growth

This goal focuses on decent work in terms of linking a person's skills to their vocation. There has been an increase in different styles of working such as working from home and remote working. This is largely due to the COVID-19 pandemic altering people's lifestyle. In addition, there is an emphasis on full and productive employment. Often people are working part-time or on a casual basis when they want full-time work. Moreover, with the knowledge economy there has been a need for additional service workers. This has led to a need for more courses related to specific topics such as education and innovation.

Industry, innovation and infrastructure

This goal relates to industry, innovation and infrastructure. It is important that regions build resilient infrastructure in terms of acquiring new technology. Due to the COVID-19 pandemic, regions have emphasised the need for independence in terms of having the appropriate infrastructures. This can then lead to more inclusive and sustainable industrialisation processes. As a result, there is expected to be a growth in innovation rates.

Reduced inequalities

This goal relates to reduced inequalities within and amongst countries. There has been increased attention placed on the difference between those living in urban and rural areas. This is due to many specific services only being available in certain locations. As a consequence, there has been policy initiatives around focusing on building new infrastructure in less developed areas.

Inequality can be measured and analysed in different ways. It can relate to educational opportunities in terms of access to learning opportunities or access to Internet and related technology infrastructure that is required for business needs. It can refer to the cost of living requirements such as the average house price.

Sustainable cities and communities

This goal focuses on how to make places sustainable, which means incorporating social, economic and environmental goals. Increasingly places are focusing on sustainability initiatives such as recycling and reusing material due to increased emphasis on land usage. This is becoming important as people live in urban areas and there is an associated interest in multi-use land usages. As a consequence, local and regional governments have been focusing on how to manage the resource usage in their area.

Many sustainability initiatives are prioritising inclusivity with regards to the access to services. This is due to an ageing population meaning many people have mobility issues but also a general concern about their work/life balance. This means safety of citizens is being a key issue in many government initiatives.

Resilience is another issue that is being prioritised in cities. This is due to the impact of the COVID-19 pandemic influencing the economic performance of regions. Due to working and studying from home requirements many regions were completely transformed. Previously prosperous cities were left vacant and only now are people slowly coming back to city areas. Therefore, regions need to develop resilience strategies in order to be able to adjust and pivot in times of crisis.

As part of the resilient strategies being developed is a focus on infrastructure in terms of access to essential services such as public transportation. Having convenient access to public transport such as trains and trams is considered important to society. This influences the ability of people to travel to different destinations.

Responsible consumption and production

This goal relates to responsible consumption and production of goods and services. In the past many goods were produced for a one-time usage but this has changed. Second hand and recycled products are now being utilised as a way of cutting down waste. This is emphasised by the amount of food that is wasted and could be used in other ways. Therefore, the usage of chemicals and other materials is now being more scrutinised.

Waste can be evaluated in terms of actual material not utilised in the production of other products. The circular economy concept has become popular as a way of encouraging the reuse and recycling of materials. In a circular economy the inputs then become outputs in other areas with the cycle then being reversed. This helps decrease pollution levels and encourages innovation.

The concept of frugal innovation in terms of making something in a more cost-efficient manner is becoming popular. This helps ensure people around the world have access to products and services regardless of their income level. The affordability of certain new products has become an issue in society particularly in developing countries.

The amount of electronic waste produced by society is being scrutinised. This is due to more people producing electronic waste and waste associated with electronic gadgets. For this reason, multiple usage recharging devices and electronic cords are being preferred. This will help to decrease the amount of electronic waste that society is producing.

Climate action

This goal relates to climate action in terms of taking action to tackle climate change. Many countries have faced rising temperatures that have altered land conditions. This has flow-on effects in terms of living conditions and also agricultural production. There has been a global increase in greenhouse gas emissions that have led to higher levels of pollution. As a consequence, there has been an emphasis on renewable energy such as wind and solar power as it does not pollute as much.

The priority areas regarding climate change focus on food security and production. This is due to changing climate conditions making land unsuitable for farming. Thus, there has been a focus on new farming methods that use less water and are more efficient. This includes focusing on the use of terrestrial and wetland ecosystems. These habitats are important for food production and also for wildlife conservation.

Freshwater deposits are important for many countries as they provide a source of drinking water. These freshwater reserves can be natural but might be impacted by surrounding regional development. This means regional and local planners need to be careful to maintain the ecological conditions of these areas. This will enable human health conditions to improve.

Life below water

The life below water goal focuses on conserving the use of water reserves for future generations. This is important due to a large percentage of the earth being classified as ocean. As a consequence, there are many marine resources that need to be protected. There has been an increase in ocean pollution due to increased wastage from people entering the ocean. Thus, many countries are now banning single-use plastic items to try to reduce wastage. The ocean has warmed that has led to alteration in marine life. In addition, changes in the water quality such as acidification have influenced the conditions of marine life.

Life on land

The life on land goal refers to the sustainable use of land in order to preserve it for future generations. Land is used for a variety of reasons including for farming and agricultural purposes. Some land has been reclaimed in order to extend city districts. This means regions need to reverse land degradation by taking care of the land. They can do this by replanting trees and taking care of the surrounding area. This can halt biodiversity loss and safeguard areas. Many animals have been threatened with extinction due to deforestation. This is particularly evident in the Amazon but also other forest areas. In addition, the loss of trees influence oxygen levels so it is important that cities have surrounding forest reserves.

Peace, justice and strong institutions

This goal focuses on the preservation of peace in society. Due to recent conflicts such as the one occurring in Ukraine with Russia, there has been an increased emphasis on peace. This can help increase a person's longevity and overall quality of life. More emphasis is being placed on providing access to services for all people regardless of income level. This enables a fairer and equitable society. By doing so entities at all levels of society are held accountable for their actions.

Partnerships for the goals

This goal focuses on implementing partnerships that can help solve problems in society. Partnerships can take on a variety of forms including public/private partnerships. Thereby enabling a way to encourage collaboration between businesses and government entities. This allows for different kinds of funding arrangements to take place.

Checklist

1. Focus on a key sustainable development goal.
2. Read previous research on sustainable development goals.
3. Incorporate facts and statistics related to the sustainable development goals. Research may have direct and indirect linkages to sustainable development goals.
4. Incorporate references related to the sustainable development goals.
5. Make sure adequate linkages exist between your research and the sustainable development goals are evident in the discussion. Can be difficult to align the research to specific sustainable development goals.

Research engagement and impact

Research involves creating new knowledge so as to add to the existing body of knowledge on a subject. Most new forms of research involve using existing knowledge in a creative way. This enables a better understanding of existing and emerging phenomenon. As the business environment constantly changes it is important that research is conducted in order to assess the changes.

Research engagement involves the interaction between a compiled body of knowledge and society. The end users of research include citizens, industry, non-government organisations, the government amongst others. Each has their own view of research and its importance. Their view will be dependent on how they perceive research influences their everyday and long-term activity. Some forms of research have immediate effects whilst other research has a more long-term effect. This means it is important to keep an open mind as to how research changes current and future thinking. To have a positive effect the research needs to foster mutually beneficial exchanges.

Research impact concerns research that has a direct and indirect impact on society. There are new ways research impact is measured. This includes the business or economic effects as well as societal impact. Research should be relevant in terms of examining issues that others are concerned with at the current point in time.

Engaging in impactful research

Researchers need to plan a strategy of engaging in impactful research whilst not compromising on scholarly needs. This means considering the type of research they are engaging in by thinking about whether it is pure or applied research. Some research might be more suited to academic journals whilst other types of research is consulting based.

It is important to have a research strategy in order to plan research studies. A strategy also helps align the goals of a study with progress made. This enables key objectives to be met that align with career development needs. This means putting into place steps needed to be taken in order to achieve the goals. A strategy is better than an ad-hoc or random path as it enables progress to be mapped. If there is no strategy in place then the path taken might be more of a serendipitous nature.

EXERCISE

Choose one of your favourite businesses and think about how they could be more sustainable.

Academic entrepreneurship

Academic entrepreneurship occurs when an academic is involved in innovative, proactive and risk-taking activity. It is often done as a way to capitalise on knowledge acquired through research activities. Research plays a dynamic role in facilitating knowledge acquisition and dissemination. Entrepreneurship typically occurs through the existence of new business ideas. It can involve a mindset in which individuals focus on trying new things. This helps to transform society by altering existing conditions.

The three main categories of academic entrepreneurship are corporate venturing, innovation and strategic renewal (Brennan & McGowan, 2006). Corporate venturing can include internal and external collaboration. Examples of internal collaboration include research centres aimed at focusing on how to solve a problem or the creation of a spin-off venture. These types of ventures are aimed at new ways of commercialising knowledge. This can be conducted with the help of a technology or science park. External ventures are collaborations aimed at connecting a business to others in the community. This enables an idea to gain momentum by incorporating the help and feedback of others. This can be conducted via a joint venture or other type of partnership.

Innovation can take on a variety of forms as long as it relates to a business kind of change. Academics often innovate through their teaching and research activities. The innovation can occur in a number of different ways but can include process innovation in terms of how things are taught and/or service innovation in terms of where and how students learn. Academics can be innovative by creating new teaching materials that are then licensed or copyrighted to others. To do this it helps to have industry liaison offices that can manage the utilisation of intellectual property.

Strategic renewal activities can include a range of knowledge transfer schemes designed to exchange information. This helps in creating communities of practice around a specific topic. Thereby enabling others to learn by example and improve overall research effectiveness.

EXERCISE

What is the difference between each sustainable development goal? Which sustainable development goals do you think best suits your research?

Guidelines

1. Before starting any research project consider thinking about which sustainable development goals can be incorporated.
2. Try to focus on one main sustainable development goal.

3. Consider whether different sustainable development goals can be incorporated at different times in the research process.
4. Highlight how your research fits with a specific sustainable development goal.
5. Try to think about incorporating questions related to the sustainable development goals in your research.

Developing expertise

Go onto the United Nations sustainable development goals web page on a frequent basis and read recently posted information.

Pitch

Develop a 2–3 minute pitch about why the sustainable development goals should be incorporated into business management research.

Suggested activities

Try to find some articles related to a topic you are interested in that mention specific sustainable development goals. Think about how the author(s) have linked the research to each goal.

Web exercise

Type into the search query a specific sustainable development goal and an industry context to find out what results appear.

Conclusion

This chapter has discussed how the sustainable development goals can be incorporated into business management studies. Each of the goals were examined in terms of their relevancy to business management studies. This enabled a way to understand how sustainability is an important part of business management research.

Review questions

1. What are the United Nations sustainable development goals?
2. Why is it useful to embed some of the sustainable development goals in your research?
3. What are two or three of the most relevant sustainable development goals associated with your research?

Multiple choice questions

1. How many sustainable development goals are there?
   a. 1
   b. 2
   c. 17
   d. 5
2. The first and second sustainable development goals refer to:
   a. No poverty and zero hunger
   b. Good health and wellbeing
   c. Quality education
   d. None of the above
3. Goal 4 about quality education refers to:
   a. Ending poverty
   b. Zero hunger
   c. Emphasising knowledge acquisition through different kinds of learning activities
   d. None of the above
4. Goal 5 about gender equality refers to:
   a. Trying to achieve gender equity
   b. Increasing participation rates of different genders
   c. Empowering both genders
   d. All of the above
5. Goal 6 about clean water and sanitation is important because
   a. Due to health effects
   b. Decreasing pollution levels
   c. None of the above
   d. All of the above

Answers: 1. c, 2. a, 3. c, 4. d, 5. d.

References

Avelar, A. B. A., da Silva-Oliveira, K. D., & da Silva Pereira, R. (2019). Education for advancing the implementation of the sustainable development goals: A systematic approach. *The International Journal of Management Education*, *17*(3), 100322.

Bali Swain, R., & Yang-Wallentin, F. (2020). Achieving sustainable development goals: Predicaments and strategies. *International Journal of Sustainable Development & World Ecology*, *27*(2), 96–106.

Brennan, M., & McGowan, P. (2006). Academic entrepreneurship: An exploratory case study. *International Journal of Entrepreneurial Behaviour & Research*, *12*(3), 144–164.

Dana, L. P., & Ratten, V. (2017). International entrepreneurship in resource-rich landlocked African countries. *Journal of International Entrepreneurship*, *15*(4), 416–435.

Di Vaio, A., Palladino, R., Hassan, R., & Escobar, O. (2020). Artificial intelligence and business models in the sustainable development goals perspective: A systematic literature review. *Journal of Business Research*, *121*, 283–314.

Giannetti, B. F., Agostinho, F., Eras, J. C., Yang, Z., & Almeida, C. M. V. B. (2020). Cleaner production for achieving the sustainable development goals. *Journal of Cleaner Production, 271*, 122127.

Hickel, J. (2019). The contradiction of the sustainable development goals: Growth versus ecology on a finite planet. *Sustainable Development, 27*(5), 873–884.

Mio, C., Panfilo, S., & Blundo, B. (2020). Sustainable development goals and the strategic role of business: A systematic literature review. *Business Strategy and the Environment, 29*(8), 3220–3245.

Moyer, J. D., & Hedden, S. (2020). Are we on the right path to achieve the sustainable development goals? *World Development, 127*, 104749.

Rashid, S., & Ratten, V. (2020). A systematic literature review on women entrepreneurship in emerging economies while reflecting specifically on SAARC countries. In: Vanessa Ratten (Ed.), *Entrepreneurship and Organizational Change*, 37–88. Heidelberg: Springer.

Ratten, V., & Ferreira, J. J. (2017). Future research directions for cultural entrepreneurship and regional development. *International Journal of Entrepreneurship and Innovation Management, 21*(3), 163–169.

Schroeder, P., Anggraeni, K., & Weber, U. (2019). The relevance of circular economy practices to the sustainable development goals. *Journal of Industrial Ecology, 23*(1), 77–95.

Van der Waal, J. W., & Thijssens, T. (2020). Corporate involvement in sustainable development goals: Exploring the territory. *Journal of Cleaner Production, 252*, 119625.

Further reading

Chankseliani, M., & McCowan, T. (2021). Higher education and the sustainable development goals. *Higher Education, 81*(1), 1–8.

Esquivel, V., & Sweetman, C. (2016). Gender and the sustainable development goals. *Gender & Development, 24*(1), 1–8.

Fleming, A., Wise, R. M., Hansen, H., & Sams, L. (2017). The sustainable development goals: A case study. *Marine Policy, 86*, 94–103.

Hák, T., Janoušková, S., & Moldan, B. (2016). Sustainable development goals: A need for relevant indicators. *Ecological Indicators, 60*, 565–573.

Katila, P., Colfer, C. J. P., De Jong, W., Galloway, G., Pacheco, P., & Winkel, G. (Eds.). (2019). *Sustainable Development Goals*. Cambridge: Cambridge University Press.

Le Blanc, D. (2015). Towards integration at last? The sustainable development goals as a network of targets. *Sustainable Development, 23*(3), 176–187.

Robert, K. W., Parris, T. M., & Leiserowitz, A. A. (2005). What is sustainable development? Goals, indicators, values, and practice. Environment: Science and Policy for Sustainable D*evelopment, 47*(3), 8–21.

10

ARTIFICIAL INTELLIGENCE AND MACHINE LEARNING

Introduction

This chapter discusses the role of artificial intelligence and machine learning in research. Increasing importance is being placed on emerging technologies that can help researchers collect and analyse data. This is due to the efficiencies obtained from the use of artificial intelligence and better data analytics.

Learning objectives

- To understand the role of artificial intelligence in research.
- To acknowledge how research studies are changing based on emerging technology.
- To examine how to incorporate artificial intelligence and machine learning in research.

> **DISCUSSION QUESTION**
>
> Why do you think the use of artificial intelligence is important in business management research?

Origins of artificial intelligence

Artificial intelligence as a term emerged at a Dartmouth College workshop discussing the role of machines in mimicking human functions (Nilsson, 2010).

DOI: 10.4324/9781003314516-10

The topic of technology replicating human activity has had a long history as indicated in different philosophies and mythologies. Due to technological advances and computing capabilities artificial intelligence will transform business management practices (De Bruyn et al., 2020). There has been much discussion around the ethical, moral and legal implications of artificial intelligence (Feng et al., 2021). This is due to the automated processes machines are now able to do. As a result, artificial intelligence is changing how customers and businesses interact.

Artificial intelligence involves some kind of reasoning process that is similar to human behaviour (Russell & Norvig, 2016). This means a technology-based system thinks like a human and is able to make decisions (Kumar et al., 2019). Thereby thinking in a rational way in terms of storing then utilising information. Artificial intelligence is defined as "the study of knowledge representations (generally) by way of computers and the use of those representations in language performance, reasoning, learning and problem solving" (Sowa, 1984:22). To be considered as artificial intelligence there needs to be some kind of knowledge representation and automated reasons (Verma et al., 2021). This will enable conclusions to be made based on the available information.

Artificial intelligence is able to adapt to new situations and find patterns. Due to the availability of big data and cheaper computing costs, there has been an increase in artificial intelligence. Artificial intelligence can be used in a range of contexts but is often used for marketing research purposes. Huang and Rust (2021) suggest that in marketing artificial intelligence can be analysed in four main ways: (1) technical algorithms that solve problems, (2) customers' psychological reactions, (3) effect on jobs and society and (4) managerial and strategic issues.

At the moment most data is collected from surveys and interviews, which require formalisation in terms of asking respondents about their participation. This kind of data has changed with more individualised and immediate data being able to be obtained through emerging technology. The disadvantage of this kind of data is that it can be delayed through bureaucratic requirements that lessen its impact. Thus, the data can be out of context and not reliable due to changing environmental trends. Emerging data practices are using artificial intelligence in the form of sensors and wearables that enable more detailed information to be obtained. This enables the acquisition of more unstructured data that can lead to more diverse findings. A way to consider the influence of artificial intelligence on research practices is to consider its content through analysis techniques. Content analysis is a way to examine information in order to assess its benefits. It was traditionally done in a manual way by focusing on different ways information can be portrayed. With the advance of new technology content analysis has moved to a computer-aided format.

Often artificial intelligence takes the form of natural language processing that uses human language to process dialogs through computers. This method enables naturally occurring words and phrases to be analysed in a technology context. It

TABLE 10.1 Advantages and disadvantages of artificial intelligence research

Advantages	*Disadvantages*
1. Can be quicker to do analysis using artificial intelligence.	1. Requires new knowledge to be obtained about artificial intelligence.
2. Enables prediction-led research results.	2. Can result in more complex data that needs different types of analysis techniques.
3. Can provide more detailed results.	3. Highlights the importance of continually learning that can be time consuming.
4. Allows for longitudinal data to be collected.	4. Requires investment in new technology.
5. Can yield new findings.	5. Can be difficult to coordinate.

is used to interpret text in a semantic way but does not analyse the context. This means it can be difficult to interpret data without knowing why and how the language is being used by others. Table 10.1 states some advantages and disadvantages of artificial intelligence research.

Digital transformation of research

There has been a digital transformation of research activities with more data collected and analysed through digital technology. This trend has been a critical factor in influencing the next wave of research methodology innovation. Contemporary research methodologies have begun to add innovative techniques such as artificial intelligence and machine learning. This has enabled cutting-edge and modern technologies to be utilised in research practices.

Research methodology practices are becoming more automated in terms of using intelligent systems. This form of new-age methods has had a positive impact on the experiences and outcomes of researchers. Technological innovations have produced a change in data collection and analysis methods and strongly asserted that research methods can work with artificial intelligence. The potential for new kinds of research findings is enormous when technology is utilised in a different way. Innovative artificial intelligence enabled systems can rapidly adapt to the needs of researchers. This enables them to come up with solution packages that tie into stakeholder needs. Business management researchers have been amongst the first to utilise artificial intelligence processes in their research activities.

Artificial intelligence generally refers to the use of intelligence by machines. This broad definition acknowledges that it needs to incorporate information systems but also knowledge acquisition. This means that a machine can sense and seize on knowledge opportunities in the market environment. By doing so they are behaving like a human in terms of reacting to the environment.

> **EXERCISE**
>
> Choose a local restaurant in your area and think about how robots can be used to make and serve food.

Artificial intelligence and human interaction

At the moment artificial intelligence is mostly used in conjunction with human interaction. However, there will be a time when artificial intelligence is at a level that supports its independent usage. This is due to artificial intelligence normally being referred to as a multifaceted concept that focuses on computer and human interaction. Artificial intelligence is increasingly affecting most functions of research practices. This includes research experience to information collection to decision-making processes. The role of artificial intelligence in research will grow in stature as it becomes more sophisticated. It can be used in different ways depending on the researchers' objectives. For example, it is often used in marketing research to obtain strategic information. This type of practice is referred to as marketing artificial intelligence as it focuses on the interaction between marketing actions and outcomes.

Marketing artificial intelligence is defined as "the development of artificial agents that given the information they have about consumers, competitors, and the focal company, suggest and/or take marketing actions to achieve the best marketing outcome" (Overgoor et al., 2019: 157). Most research related to marketing is affected in some degree by the use of artificial intelligence. This includes collecting real-time and relevant information from different sources such as customers, businesses and government entities. Artificial intelligence in marketing research makes it more easier to obtain information but on the flip side makes it more difficult to analyse.

> **EXERCISE**
>
> What kind of artificial intelligence do you think will be used by researchers in the next 10, 50 and 100 years? How do you think artificial intelligence will evolve in society?

ARTICLE READING ANALYSIS

Read the following article about the use of artificial intelligence in research studies.

- Lévesque, M., Obschonka, M., & Nambisan, S. (2022). Pursuing impactful entrepreneurship research using artificial intelligence. *Entrepreneurship Theory and Practice, 46*(4), 803–832.

Consider why leading-edge artificial intelligence can transform entrepreneurship to be more business relevant.

Types of digital technologies

The main emerging digital technologies can be classified into three main categories: digital artefact, digital platform and digital infrastructure (Rippa & Secundo, 2019). Digital artefacts include augmented reality, blockchain, conversation system, digital storytelling, digital business portfolio and virtual reality (Rippa & Secundo, 2019). Digital storytelling involves telling stories through digital platforms. This can include using multimedia such as audio and video that makes the story more interactive. The benefit of digital storytelling is that it enables the use of images that can help a person understand the story being told. It also makes it more interesting and interactive as related material such as music and graphics can be shown whilst explaining a story.

Digital business portfolio involves a collection of digital artefacts that are collated by a person. Each artefact is used to support the expertise of the creator. Examples of artefacts can include online presentations and web pages that showcase a person's work. Virtual and augmented reality involves technologies that enable a person to interact in a Web-based environment. By doing so it enables a person to transform how they utilise technology and to create maker believe environments.

Conversational system involves utilising technology to make conversations with others. Typically this is done through chatbots that facilitate computer-generated questions and answers. Blockchain is a digital record of transactions made through cryptocurrencies. It is increasingly being used as a way to transact bitcoin and is globally traded. The advantage of blockchain is that it offers a disintermediated financial service. Digital platforms include intelligence apps, service architecture, cloud computing, big data, learning analytics and social media (Rippa & Secundo, 2019).

Machine learning

Machine learning is defined as "a process by which computers are trained using available data in making advanced decisions similar to the human thinking process"

(Arachchige et al., 2022:6). Machine learning can handle more complex data analysis including nonlinear relationships. This means it is often used as a way to understand intercorrelations amongst variables. Arachchige et al. (2022) suggest that a machine learning method involves data processing when all the data is transferred into machine learning fields. This can include creating dummy variables for categorical variables and scaling all variables (Arachchige et al., 2022). Once this has been done the data can then be split so that it can be better tested. The next step involves hyperparameter tuning in which the model for each parameter set is estimated. This leads to a calculation about the importance of each variable. Then the data is updated and the model is evaluated.

Immersive technologies

Immersive technologies include artificial intelligence, augmented reality, mixed reality and digital humans (Sung et al., 2022). Artificial intelligence is defined as "systems that mimic human personalities and characteristics, with capabilities to engage in human-like speech, learning and problem solving" (Sung et al., 2022:1). Artificial intelligence can enhance research practices by increasing the accuracy of data collection. It can help design meaningful research experiences that better align with expectations.

Artificial intelligence transforms research practices into more engaging interactions between the investigator and participants of a study. Artificial intelligence can include avatars and virtual bots that are designed to interact with humans. Increasingly robots are used to communicate with humans or to do certain tasks. Due to the COVID-19 pandemic, the interest in robots because of social distancing and hygiene requirements has increased. At the same time computing has become more sophisticated and enabled better types of robots.

Artificial intelligence utilises computing technology to recognise human instructions. This includes using digital content such as audio and graphics to answer human queries. It is an interaction process and is designed to mimic the real environment. Mixed reality refers to a singular immersive reality that combines the physical and virtual world. It is increasingly being used in society due to its usefulness in facilitating technology-embedded experiences. In research studies mixed reality is used to integrate digital technologies into research experiences. Mixed reality enables researchers to incorporate real-life experiences such as virtually visiting places in order to ask research questions. This means it can be a more cheaper and cost-effective way to do research.

In research studies digital humans are used as they represent a way to utilise technology that has a human appearance. Digital humans can engage in interviews and express emotions. They can offer a more friendly and technological way to do research. Digital humans can recognise speech and respond to environmental changes. This means researchers utilise digital humans in order to develop new research strategies.

Storytelling

Storytelling is a research technique designed to share information with respondents. It can be done with applied technology that combines artificial intelligence with entertainment. Thereby communicating information with individuals through an interactive format. The benefit of using digital storytelling is that it creates a technology-enhanced research environment.

Narrating a story can trigger a person's thought processes making it easier to respond to information. The concept of storytelling is frequently used in business management studies due to the way it invokes emotional responses. This means it can yield better insights into experiences. Applying storytelling in research can create better relationships with participants.

Stories can be used in one-time research studies or longitudinal studies depending on the nature of the study. Storytelling is utilised as a highly effective way to communicate the rationale and purpose of a study. This means it can be used to convince participants to engage in the research study experience.

In the past storytelling was done through verbal or written communication. This has changed with the use of immersive technologies such as augmented and mixed reality. Azuma (2015) suggests that reality-enhanced technology storytelling can be used in terms of reinforcing, reskinning and remembering. Reinforcing refers to highlighting the place or event that is being researched. This occurs when it is not possible to directly engage in the context and it needs to be restated in a way others understand. Sung et al. (2022:2) state that reskinning refers to "redefining objects for the purpose of the digital story". This means the objects are changed in order to suit the context of the study. Remembering means referring to a context that occurred in the past. This can involve retelling stories by linking the context to where the event took place. Thereby triggering a person's memory in terms of the emotions associated with the event.

Neurophysiological research methods

The main methods to measure neurological responses are "electroencephalography (EEG, event-related potentials (ERPs), functional magnetic resonance imaging (fMRI), functional near-infrared spectroscopy (fNIRS), magnetoencephalography (MEG), positron emission tomography (PET), steady state topography (SST) and transcranial magnetic stimulation (TMS)" (Zhang et al., 2022:1). Neurological response methods involve examining how people change based on recording neural activities. They can be measured in a direct and indirect way depending on the nature of the change.

There has been a strong growth in neurophysical research methods in recent years. This is due to a need by researchers to understand the impact of different stimuli. This has led to a reliance on self-report methods in which an individual mentions their responses. Self-report methods depend on the willingness and capability of people to detail their responses. This can be hard to do due to time issues as well as emotional needs. Whilst self-report methods provide valuable data, there is a need to obtain more objective and timely responses. This is due to many people not understanding their behaviours and not being able to report it. As a consequence, much behaviour including unconscious processes are not reported. This means new research methods are required that analyse a person's unconscious processes.

There are often social pressures associated with self-reports that negate the validity of individual responses. This means that a person will express certain responses due to a need to conform to societal expectations. This can lead to biased findings and misleading results.

Neuromarketing or consumer neuroscience is defined as "the use of neurological or biological methods of marketing and consumer research" (Zhang et al., 2022: 1). It is gaining recognition as a way to add value to studies due to the way it reports reactions. This enables emotions and decisions to be measured in a more specific way. The advantage of neuromarketing tools is that they focus on the needs and values of research studies. This enables spontaneous and unrehearsed responses to be obtained. Neurophysiological methods help in obtaining hidden information that might not be known by respondents.

EEG and ERP

EEG involves measuring "the modulation of brainwaves, which are characterised into five spectral bands based on different frequencies: Delta (0–4Hz), Theta (4–8Hz), Alpha (8–12Hz), Beta (12–30 Hz) and Gamma (above 30Hz)" (Zhang et al., 2022: 2). The goal of EEG is to record changes of electrical signals that occur when individuals are exposed to different conditions. EEG detects the intensity of the change that might be hard to directly observe. The advantage of EEG is that it can detect different electrical differences that provide information about brain processing. This means emotions can be measured through the generation of neurons on the scalp. This means a range of brain activities in terms of decision-making and responses can be recorded.

EEG can be conducted for a relatively low cost based on how much detailed information it provides. This enables the modulation of brain activity to be confirmed through cognitive behaviour. Thereby helping to understand how neuron activities change. EEG is typically used to understand subconscious reactions that are often spontaneous in nature. Thereby helping to examine real-life behaviour. ERPs can be described as "the electrical activity of neuron groups recorded on the scalp" (Zhang et al., 2022:4). This means brain activity can be measured when it is exposed to predetermined stimuli. Thereby measuring how people respond to tasks and their electrophysiological responses.

fMRI

fMRI occurs when a person lies on an MRI scanner that tracks their brain activity. The aim of fMRI is to detect alternations in brain activity. This enables more information to be obtained about neuronal activities. MRI scanners detect changes in blood oxygenation. This means when an individual is exposed to different stimuli there will be coinciding blood flow changes in the brain. This enables the MRI scanner to track the changes.

The advantage of MRI scanners is that they enable hidden activity in the brain to be analysed. This means it provides a good way to understand detailed changes. Researchers tend to use fMRI in conjunction with other methods in order to obtain more detailed results. This is due to traditional methods such as interviews relying on self-reports instead of actual neurological changes.

fNIRS

fNIRS is defined as "a non-invasive optical neuroimaging method that measures blood oxygenation underneath the superficial cortex" (Zhang et al., 2022:4). It uses probes to detect brain responses through changes in the relative hemoglobin level. The advantage of fNIRS is that it can be used in different environments due to its portable nature. This enables it to measure general brain changes.

MEG

MEG occurs when a helmet is placed on the head of a person to detect changes in brain activity. MEG is a technical way to understand changes in magnetic cerebral signals based on changes in an individual's environment. Thereby helping to understand real-time responses to stimuli. It does not have as much capabilities as fMRI but still offers an effective way to predict behaviour. Thereby enabling more information to be obtained about subtle changes. This helps detail short-term alterations in emotions.

PET

PET is a method that "tests and records gamma rays that are emitted by active biological tracer molecules that are introduced into the body of participants" (Zhang et al., 2022:4). It is an invasive method due to the way it introduces rays into a person before the environmental stimuli change. Thereby it raises ethical and moral issues as to its usage by researchers.

SST

SST utilises a head cap to record brain electronical changes. It can detect rapid as well as slow changes in brain activity. The advantage of SST is that it enables visual stimuli to be presented to an individual in order to understand their responses.

TMS

TMS is a way to understand specific locational changes in a person. Zhang et al. (2022:5) state "TMS uses one or more coils to stimulate the scalp through a magnetic field and to change the brain patterns or activities, thereby generating an electrical response that causes neurons to depolarise synchronously". This means it tests how specific brain areas change. It is easily portable meaning it can be used in a range of environments. However, it has disadvantages including radiation exposure that limit its general applicability.

Biological research methods

Research can be conducted through measuring changes in a person's biology. This includes eye tracking, facial expression analysis, skin response and heart rates. Each of these biological responses represents a way to understand how people behave in society. Thereby assisting researchers' ability to directly measure reactions.

Eye tracking

Eye tracking is a method that tracks eye movement. It is commonly used by consumer behaviour researchers to understand how and why people buy certain products. Research is done by measuring eye movement such as where a person looks and the time duration of their gaze. In addition, the sequence of the gaze is examined to understand consumer behaviour. Research can be conducted in an experimental setting or in a real-life setting. Studies are often done on eye tracking in website design. This enables websites to include relevant colours and other features that can lead to better sales.

Facial expression

Facial expression analysis measures changes in facial muscles based on alterations in the environment. This can be done based on the evaluation of different kinds of emotions such as happy, sad, worried and surprise. There are different kinds of software that can be used to measure changes in addition to facial recognition software.

Skin conductance response

Skin conductance response methods measure changes in skin electronic transmissions. This is normally done by invoking different situations or atmospheres that are measuring the changes in sweat glands. This helps in understanding how individuals' psychological state changes based on different stimuli.

Heart rate

Heart rates are a way to understand how the nervous system responds to certain stimuli. It is done by recording electrical waves that can be measured by heart rate activity. When the heart beats fast then it is likely a person is excited but if it does not change this may mean there is no reaction. Heart rate activity can be used to understand a person's emotional attachment to a product as well as certain preferences.

ARTICLE READING ANALYSIS

Read the following article about the use of artificial intelligence and big data in entrepreneurship.

- Obschonka, M., & Audretsch, D. B. (2020). Artificial intelligence and big data in entrepreneurship: a new era has begun. *Small Business Economics, 55*(3), 529–539.

Think about the disruptive potential of artificial intelligence and how this will change entrepreneurship research.

Guidelines

1. Think about how artificial intelligence can be used in your research prior to starting the research process.
2. Try to incorporate new types of artificial intelligence into your research.
3. Consider utilising machine learning in your methodology.
4. Try to think about the time and cost issues associated with the use of artificial intelligence.
5. Find out how other researchers are using artificial intelligence.

Developing expertise

Try to read one article per week that relates to artificial intelligence in order to keep up to date with new developments.

Pitch

Develop a 2–3 minute pitch that discusses how artificial intelligence can be used in research studies.

Checklist

1. Research new methods that use artificial intelligence.
2. Highlight the more detailed information obtained from artificial intelligence technology.
3. Utilise a mixed methods approach that incorporates artificial intelligence.
4. Spend time on reading and learning about artificial intelligence.
5. Hire an artificial intelligence expert to help you with the analysis.

Conclusion

This chapter has reviewed how artificial intelligence can be used in research. This means including new information and material on artificial intelligence. Thereby enabling new techniques to be utilised in research studies.

Review questions

1. What is artificial intelligence?
2. How can artificial intelligence be used in research studies?
3. What kind of new technologies are emerging that can help researchers?

Suggested activity

Design a research study that incorporates the use of artificial intelligence.

Web exercise

On the Internet type in the search query 'artificial intelligence and business management' and see what results are shown.

Multiple choice questions

1. Artificial intelligence as a term emerged at which college?
   a. Stanford
   b. Harvard
   c. Dartmouth
   d. None of the above
2. Artificial intelligence includes what kind of knowledge representations?
   a. Language performance
   b. Reasoning
   c. Learning and problem solving
   d. All of the above

3. Marketing artificial intelligence can be analysed in what way?
   a. Technical algorithms that solve problems
   b. Customers' psychological reactions
   c. Managerial issues
   d. All of the above
4. The five different frequencies to measure the modulation of brainwaves through EEG are:
   a. Sea, wind, water, air, land
   b. Delta, theta, alpha, beta and gamma
   c. All of the above
   d. None of the above
5. ERP is the abbreviation for
   a. Event related potential
   b. Equal running potential
   c. Enduring related plans
   d. None of the above

Answers

1. C, 2. D, 3. D, 4. B., 5. A

References

Arachchige, J., Quach, S., Roca, E., Liu, B., Liew, A. W. C., & Earl, G. (2022). Understanding high-involvement product purchase through an innovative machine learning approach: A case of housing type choice. *Journal of Consumer Behaviour*, in Press.

Azuma, R. (2015). Location-based mixed and augmented reality storytelling. In *Fundamentals of Wearable Computers and Augmented Reality*: 259–276, W. Barfield (Ed.). Boca Raton: CRC Press.

De Bruyn, A., Viswanathan, V., Beh, Y. S., Brock, J. K. U., & Von Wangenheim, F. (2020). Artificial intelligence and marketing: Pitfalls and opportunities. *Journal of Interactive Marketing*, *51*(1), 91–105.

Feng, C. M., Park, A., Pitt, L., Kietzmann, J., & Northey, G. (2021). Artificial intelligence in marketing: A bibliographic perspective. *Australasian Marketing Journal*, *29*(3), 252–263.

Huang, M. H., & Rust, R. T. (2021). A strategic framework for artificial intelligence in marketing. *Journal of the Academy of Marketing Science*, *49*(1), 30–50.

Kumar, V., Rajan, B., Venkatesan, R., & Lecinski, J. (2019). Understanding the role of artificial intelligence in personalized engagement marketing. *California Management Review*, *61*(4), 135–155.

Lévesque, M., Obschonka, M., & Nambisan, S. (2022). Pursuing impactful entrepreneurship research using artificial intelligence. *Entrepreneurship Theory and Practice*, *46*(4), 803–832.

Nilsson, N. J. (2010). *The Quest for Artificial Intelligence: A History of Ideas and Achievements*. Cambridge: Cambridge University Press.

Obschonka, M., & Audretsch, D. B. (2020). Artificial intelligence and big data in entrepreneurship: A new era has begun. *Small Business Economics*, *55*(3), 529–539.

Overgoor, G., Chica, M., Rand, W., & Weishampel, A. (2019). Letting the computers take over: Using AI to solve marketing problems. *California Management Review, 61*(4), 156–185.

Rippa, P., & Secundo, G. (2019). Digital academic entrepreneurship: The potential of digital technologies on academic entrepreneurship. *Technological Forecasting and Social Change, 146*, 900–911.

Russell, S. J., & Norvig, P. (2016). *Artificial Intelligence: A Modern Approach*. Malaysia: Pearson.

Sowa, J. F. (1984). *Conceptual Structures: Information Processing in Mind and Machine*. Reading, MA: Addison-Wesley Longman Publishing.

Sung, E. C., Han, D. I. D., Bae, S., & Kwon, O. (2022). What drives technology-enhanced storytelling immersion? The role of digital humans. *Computers in Human Behavior, 132*, 107246.

Verma, S., Sharma, R., Deb, S., & Maitra, D. (2021). Artificial intelligence in marketing: Systematic review and future research direction. *International Journal of Information Management Data Insights, 1*(1), 100002.

Zhang, Y., Thaichon, P., & Shao, W. (2022). Neuroscientific research methods and techniques in consumer research. *Australasian Marketing Journal*, 14413582221085321.

Further reading

Chalmers, D., MacKenzie, N. G., & Carter, S. (2021). Artificial intelligence and entrepreneurship: Implications for venture creation in the fourth industrial revolution. *Entrepreneurship Theory and Practice, 45*(5), 1028–1053.Shepherd, D. A., & Majchrzak, A. (2022). Machines augmenting entrepreneurs: Opportunities (and threats) at the Nexus of artificial intelligence and entrepreneurship. *Journal of Business Venturing, 37*(4), 106227.

Turkina, E. (2018). The importance of networking to entrepreneurship: Montreal's artificial intelligence cluster and its born-global firm element AI. *Journal of Small Business & Entrepreneurship, 30*(1), 1–8.

INDEX

For Product Safety Concerns and Information please contact our EU
representative GPSR@taylorandfrancis.com
Taylor & Francis Verlag GmbH, Kaufingerstraße 24, 80331 München, Germany

www.ingramcontent.com/pod-product-compliance
Ingram Content Group UK Ltd.
Pitfield, Milton Keynes, MK11 3LW, UK
UKHW020001200926
475702UK00015B/2410
9781032323374